The Faces
of Post 41

The Faces of Post 41

South Phoenix Latinos fight for their country abroad, and for their civil rights at home.

By Charles H. Sanderson

Edited by Peter Madrid

Historical consultant, Dr. Pete R. Dimas

Published by Latino Perspectives Media
and the Raul Castro Institute
Phoenix, Arizona 2008

Raul H. Castro Institute
PUBLIC POLICY | EDUCATION | LEADERSHIP

Sponsored by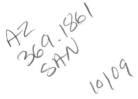

The Faces of Post 41
by Charles H. Sanderson

Published by Latino Perspectives Media

and by The Raul H. Castro Institute

Raul H. Castro Institute
PUBLIC POLICY | EDUCATION | LEADERSHIP

First edition 2008
Phoenix, Arizona

Printed in the United States of America.

ISBN # 9780615232669

Thoughts and thanks from the author

Sometimes we make history. Other times history is too much like a ghost. It fades away before we realize its beauty and its lessons. As a fifth-generation native in the Salt River Valley, I've watched our heritage become lost daily. My 90-year-old grandfather can remember riding with his family in their ramshackle 1919 Buick to downtown Phoenix for wrestling night at the Madison Square Garden. He still laughs at the horrible smell of sweat and he smiles at the cheers of excitement.

Then it was gone. And why? So much of our heritage has fallen away to wrecking balls and oversight. I don't remember any politicians leaping to save this icon. I saw only a scattered few community members cry out about the tragedy. The building was torn down, lost to neglect and sacrificed to progress. Like much of South Phoenix.

In 2005, during work on an article about one of these losses – the Golden Gate barrio – I met one of those scattered few voices; Dr. Pete R. Dimas. Not only was he fighting to save the legacy of Sacred Heart Church and give Phoenix its first Hispanic Cultural Center, he was part of a new study, the Hispanic Historic Property Survey, that hoped to save these disregarded edifices of Phoenix history before more could be lost.

One was American Legion Post 41.

Dimas, more than anyone, is responsible for helping tell the story of Post 41. It is to him and many others that I owe these pages. Cecilia Rosales of Latino Perspectives Media, and Trino Sandoval of the Raúl H. Castro Institute deserve our recognition for having helped to publish this book.

Along the way, historians, veterans, and family and friends have shared more than could be contained in so humble a book. Christine Marín, Curator/Archivist Historian and her staff at the Chicano Research Collection at Arizona State University are responsible for a majority of the photos and much of the research in this book. Commander Robert Hernandez opened the doors of Post 41, and opened the forgotten boxes of its history.

Jean Reynolds, Chandler's public-history coordinator, and Maggie Rivas-Rodriguez of the University of Texas, both have given their assistance. Charles Bugh, Post 41 commander (2007-2008) deserves thanks, as well as Rick Dimas. I thank my friends Jason and Michelle for keeping me sane in the blistering five months of this project.

But above all, I must thank Post 41. Its claim of "friendliest post in the nation" may very well be true. For sharing memories both beautiful and heartbreaking, I must show immense appreciation to the following members of Post 41: Lencho Othon, Steve Zozaya, Henry Daley Jr., Tony Valenzuela, Manny Lugo, Rudy Lopez and Adam Hernandez.

In 2008, Post 41 was presented with a certificate. Its humble building was now listed and protected as a historic property. Along with these stories, we hope that Post 41 can also stand beside the Navajo Code Talkers, Lincoln and Eleanor Ragsdale, Ira Hayes and all of Arizona's unexpected and treasured heroes. Post 41 is a part of our history and our future. It should never be forgotten.

– Charles H. Sanderson
November 5, 2008

Below, the construction
on American Legion
Post 41 nears completion.
December 22, 1947
Photo Courtesy American Legion Post 41

Table of Contents

The building is humble. Red brick. White stucco. It stands quietly like a sentry over the boundary between old South Phoenix barrios and downtown's shining skyscrapers. Many of the neighborhoods that once surrounded it are gone, turned into a baseball stadium, a massive rental car facility, airport runways and empty lots.

The building's name is long: American Legion Tony F. Soza/Ray Martinez Thunderbird Post 41.

Most days, it is low-lit inside. Visitors walk into the post's Ronda Room bar and forget the brutal summer outside. Slowly, as the day drags on, more people sit at the stools to toss back a few drinks and chat. Through a doorway, into another room, the original section of the post houses a large corner case. Resting there is the bronze bust of a founder, along with photos of war heroes, senators and the post's first flag. The room opens up into Frank Fuentes Hall, a larger area with two rows of red-brick support pillars marching up to a small stage. A blue star marks the center of the room's white floor, honoring mothers of soldiers at war. Well-worn tables line the periphery.

The walls are covered with photographs. Rows of old picture frames display the faces of past commanders. A case holds photocopied medals, ribbons, newspaper clippings and forgotten portraits. Against the back wall is a stage. It covers an old sunken bar that most members have forgotten still exists; hidden beneath the platform and used for storage. A large American flag hangs proudly onstage. Across the room and back past the brick pillars is a mural painted in 1985 on the far wall. It portrays the proud, young enlisted men and women in all the armed forces, their Latino faces aimed at the flag. The largest face, the one in the center, wears a Congressional Medal of Honor around his neck.

Nearby, two large photographs show Pima Indian Ira Hayes and Mexican American Medal of Honor recipient Silvestre Herrera. Indeed the building is filled wall to wall with faces: The faces of Post 41.

Back in the Ronda Room bar, men talk about work, family, cars and jokes they've heard. The friendships seem easy, with an unseen connection between them. They have fought in all the major battles of our time, scattered across modern history from the many fronts of World War II to Korea, Vietnam, Afghanistan and Iraq.

But the story of Post 41 is not just of the achievements of individuals in the United States Armed Forces. The story also portrays a fight for equality and the right to cherish ones' own heritage.

There are historians who might suggest that the social changes Post 41 helped to usher in were simply a sign of the times. Minorities across the U.S. had begun to enter arenas of life and enjoy opportunities that they had been barred from for much of American history. But what makes Post 41 a rare story is just how humble its roots were. These were the kids of South Phoenix; barrios that had long been ostracized, almost wholly ignored by the city around them. Most hadn't been to college. Many hadn't graduated from high school.

These "average men" from the barrios of South Phoenix fought for respect in a city that refused to acknowledge their equality. The early battles were not waged on easy roads. They were fighting for equality that had been taken decades before.

Setting the stage

Anglo arrival

"Any city however small, is in fact divided into two, one the city of the poor, the other of the rich. These are at war with one another."
– Plato, Greek philosopher

Nothing begins out of a vacuum in society. Events build slowly into the next defining moment. The formation of American Legion Post 41 is no different. Its existence, its purpose and its fight against segregation; these all existed because of the early storyline that formed the U.S. territory of Arizona, and later, the state.

In 1861, a majority of Anglo settlers to reach the region were military men sent to protect mining interests against Apache raiding parties.[1] Mexican families were also migrating north into the central valleys of Arizona from Tucson and northern Sonora throughout the 1850s and 1860s to set up farms and cattle ranches.[2]

Then, almost as soon as it had been obtained by the U.S., the region was left to fend for itself. As the Civil War detonated in April 1861, troops began to pull to the east for battle, under orders from President Abraham Lincoln.[1a] Apache Indians increased their attacks on vulnerable new settlements, ranches and mining operations across the upper Sonoran Desert, momentarily spurred in the belief they had caused the military departure.[3]

Arizona was then part of New Mexico, but too isolated to depend on its cities for protection. Requests had been made for several years to split the region into two territories. President Lincoln finally relented in 1863, making Arizona an official territory in hopes of weakening Confederate control in the area. Only the California Column and occupying forces of the Confederate Army would cross the land, often attacked by Indians as well.

A desperate plea was sent to Congress for help. The territory needed $250,000 to enlist volunteers for defense against the Apaches who continued to ravage the countryside. Their funds request was denied. The communities of Arizona were forced to go it alone. This they did.[2a]

On Sept. 2, 1865, a volunteer army was formed. Then two chaotic months were spent organizing the new outfit. Approximately 350 men were sworn in to service for one year. Together, they formed five companies of Arizona volunteers. The companies were designated A through F, excluding "D." The Arizona Army National Guard's history began that November in Tubac, when Company E began its first training exercises.

Most of the volunteers were Mexicans, Pima and Maricopa Indians, with 11 mostly Anglo officers. Indian attacks were a common struggle. Northern Sonora and Chihuahua had their own protracted and frustrating history with Apaches. With so many Mexicans in the ranks it is no surprise that as they prepared to fight off the Apaches, their motto became a Spanish word, "Cuidado!" (Be Careful!).

Settling together

In 1866, the regular troops would return to Arizona.
A former Union soldier, John Y.T. Smith, would secure a contract with the newly-constructed Fort McDowell, supplying hay to feed the horses. It wasn't hard to find workers to harvest the grass growing along the banks of the Salt River. Mexican settlers forced north were looking for extra work to supplement their incomes; their land in Mexico was beginning to fall into the possesion of land barons such as Colonel Luis Terrazas.

Many had been farming along the upper Gila River, but overgrazing and deforestation caused flash floods that decimated their crops.[4] They soon found that working with Smith was safer than other options, such as tedious labor in the mines that dotted the countryside. Living and working near Fort McDowell also provided some safety from the Apache raiding parties.

Fledgling settlements began taking shape along the banks of the Salt River. With time – and blessed with no Indian raids – Phoenix and Tempe took root. Though it was easy to see numerous 14th century Hohokam ruins dotting the landscape, Jack Swilling, a former Confederate soldier, was the first to realize ancient canals had been carved across the large Valley floor.

Below, men dig the canals that will soon turn the Salt River Valley into an farming powerhouse.

PHOTO COURTESY SALT RIVER PROJECT

In 1868 he secured the funding to form an irrigation company, enlisting Mexican labor to clear the canals and add irrigation ditches. Swilling and his Mexican wife Trinidad Escalante joined the new settlement.

As opportunities grew, more Mexicans, Indians and Anglos would converge on the untapped Valley.

Everyone pitched in to establish a community. In the remote isolation, their struggle to survive left no time for elitism, racism or segregation. Such views were largely kept in check as the town scraped an early existence out of the hard Sonoran Desert. Town Marshall Henry Garfias, a Mexican American from California, kept order in Phoenix. Supplies (and word of the outside world) arrived from Wickenburg to the north, or were shipped from Port Guaymas, Mexico, to the town of Maricopa Wells, 35 thorny miles to the south – a full day's ride by horse and wagon.

After irrigation ditches were dug in Phoenix, and as the desert began giving up its agricultural gift, a thin steel scar was being etched across the pristine Arizona landscape. Marching east from Yuma, the Southern Pacific Railroad had begun to lay its tracks in 1879. By May, it would reach Maricopa Wells.

Soon after, enterprising men such as Darrel Duppa set up teamster wagons to ferry travelers across the sea of cactus. When the Chinese Exclusion Act of 1882 took away one labor force, a new one was hired. Mexican laborers filled the void of Chinese workers, helping to add new rail lines throughout the Southwest. Nine years after the railroad came to Arizona, 87 Mexican workers began grading a roadbed for a new line of track between Maricopa Wells and Phoenix, slowly closing the gap between the Valley and the outside world. As summer months blistered the countryside, work halted and the Mexican labor force drifted into Phoenix, seeking light work until

The Maricopa & Phoenix Railroad train rolls into the new station at Phoenix, 24 miles from its departure in Maricopa Wells.

the heat passed. Such was the migratory life of Mexican labor in the early days of Arizona. They followed the work.

When the first iron horse steamed into Phoenix at dawn on July 4th, 1887, as part of the Maricopa & Phoenix Railroad, it brought more than what could be imagined. Now that travel was easier, the last American frontiers were about to fill up, displace cultures and change the U.S. forever. The world's largest land-grab, under the premise of Manifest Destiny, was coming to an end.

With the trains came people and supplies from the Eastern U.S. and from California. Port Guaymas was no longer a main supply line. The Mexican thread of culture began to weaken as the Anglo communities in Phoenix enjoyed new luxuries and found free time to express ideas that had been set aside. The tenuous multicultural existence faded, and so began the scourge of segregation and prejudiced ideals.

The tracks were an unsightly mark on the land, noisy with the coming and going of trains, people and supplies. The area was seen as undesirable to arriving Anglos, and land values south of town faltered. Slowly, laws and city ordinances began to appear, segregating communities both blatantly and with subtlety. Land barons such as Michael Wormser arrived on the scene to snatch up property where they could. Poor and displaced families began to collect into areas they could afford, mainly around the train tracks south of town.

By 1885, the Mexican and Mexican American population within Phoenix had dropped to a quarter of the total population as more Anglos arrived and the Mexican population moved into rural farmland across the Valley. Land was sold cheap by farmers hoping to tie down the inexpensive, but migratory Mexican labor force.

Then a defining moment set the future in motion.

A flood of change

On Feb. 19, 1891, winter storms raged across Arizona, bringing change. The problems began at 1 a.m., announced by telegraph. An engineer was sending word from the Arizona Dam, 25 miles up the Salt River. Water had begun to spill over the dam and was rising fast. Phoenix's Marshall "Billy" Blankenship was awaken from his sleep to gather men and warn anyone living closest to the river. As families fled to high ground with what little they could carry, the floodwaters rose, eating away at the banks of the river.

As predawn approached, the crowds tried to ignore the dissolving walls of adobe homes being sucked down into the torrent. They talked over the occasional crash of metal. Crowds milled about in the brisk air and moonlight, joking nervously as sickening sounds of wreckage drifted over the rush of water. When the sun finally crept up past the horizon, the flood came into full view. Several homes were gone – others clung perilously to islands that had resisted erosion. The railroad bridge had fallen at about 5 a.m. along with a mile of track ripped loose in the collapse. The telegraph line and poles were washed away as well, severing contact with the outside world. All that remained was "one iron span that still clung quivering and unsteadily to the south bank of Salt River."[5]

It would be almost a week before the floods finally receded, leaving roads as far north as Washington Street awash in mud and silt. Few lives were lost, but on the waterlogged banks of the Salt River, the story of South Phoenix had begun.

Those who could afford new homes moved to higher ground and began the northward expansion of Phoenix that continues today. Those who could not were forced to live in the decimated communities nearest the Salt River. The Mexican barrios began to take shape. They were also populated by Chinese, Blacks, prostitutes – anyone forced to live at risk in the now-affordable floodplain.

With no building codes to govern construction, homes were built out of adobe bricks and spare wood. The roofs were thatched. Most had dirt floors that led out to dirt yards and dirt streets. There was no water or sewer system, save the occasional outhouse. Many of these communities would remain largely unchanged for the next 60 years, most outside Phoenix city limits until 1959. It would take years to pour concrete floors for their homes, and for activists to convince city officials to finally bring street lights, pavement and sidewalks in the 1960s.

As the new century approached, businesses began to build factories on the now-affordable land. But as time passed the land became polluted and people began to see clear dividing lines. A grey area formed between Van Buren and the railroad tracks built only a few years before.

Latinos were not welcome north of Van Buren, and it was seldom to see any well-to-do Anglo venture farther south than the train tracks. Though decades in the making, this was the world into which Ray Martinez and Frank "Pipa" Fuentes were born.

The flood of 1891, looking toward "A" Mountain, from the north side of the Salt River in Tempe.

The dividing line

"Washington was a dividing line. We could go up and down Washington Street and we ... couldn't go into the theatre, except in the balcony ... there were three theatres we could, and the others we couldn't. But we could go in and buy ice cream.

"But north, like say Adams or Van Buren, noooo. That was off limits. That was no-man's land for us. You didn't dare. You could go up there. But not to try to buy anything." – Ray Martinez, co-founder of Post 41[6]

In 1891, after the Salt River returned to normal, the land around its banks became the last place any investor wanted to spend money, even though real estate was a major source of the economy at the time. Few real estate promoters cared to undertake any residential development in flood-prone areas.[7]

Indeed, to confirm this distaste, two more floods would inundate the area in 1906 and 1908 before the Roosevelt Dam was built in 1911 and the river finally choked off.

Land was sold cheap for the construction of factories, flour mills, warehouses and stockyards. The desirability of land in the area dropped further. Another industry that flourished in South Phoenix was agriculture. Many Mexican farmers had worked the area but, in a twist of irony, the 1891 flood was followed by a decade of drought. Water soon became a rare commodity. Banks and land barons took control of the precious irrigation water. Then Anglo farmers and ranchers such as Dwight Heard took over the acreages and hired the land-stripped Mexican farmers to work their own land and livestock for cheap wages. Anglos had begun to rule daily life in the Valley.

Real estate salesmen were frustrated by Heard as he undercut their profits in the farmland south of town. To retaliate, they would launch a slander campaign that further solidified the bad reputation of the area.

Meanwhile, frustration began to boil over in Mexico among rural communities that had felt abused by their government and by land barons that had slowly pushed Mexicans north. The frustration sparked The Mexican Revolution, which drove even more Mexican nationals north. Between 1911 and 1920 more than 890,000 Mexican citizens legally entered the U.S. seeking safety.

Migrant laborers at a temporary cotton camp in 1930s Tolleson.

PHOTO COURTESY ARIZONA HISTORICAL SOCIETY

The unofficial number must have been higher as Mexican nationals flooded the Southwestern U.S., fleeing the bullets flying on their own soil. Various Mexican revolutionary actions such as the "Plan de San Diego" sparked absurd fears among Anglos that they would be next. Rumors of an intercepted plot to take over Phoenix in 1914 only added to Anglo distrust of the Mexican population.[8]

Despite these fears, Anglo farmers still needed Mexican labor to work their fields. With the start of President

Theodore Roosevelt's Federal Reclamation Act in 1902 and the formation of the Salt River Project in 1903, the Salt River Valley's agricultural industry was exploding. Cotton would soon bring even more Mexican laborers north in search of work. By 1912, as mining activity slowed in Arizona, the irrigated fields of central Arizona took over the economy, fed by the new reservoir at Roosevelt Dam. Cotton farms quilted the desert landscape as the Salt River Valley began to surpass Cotton Belt plantations in the Southeastern U.S. In 1914, the Salt River Valley boasted the world's best Egyptian cotton.

With 186,000 acres of cotton in the Salt River Valley alone, Arizona had undeniably become one of the largest cotton producers in the U.S.

During World War I, as Anglo workers turned to the war effort, farms found a need for more hands. To supply labor, farmers pushed to bring still more Mexican hands north. When the war ended, the Mexican and Mexican American population continued to grow through the 1920s.

With the success of agriculture, Hispanic barrios began to sprout next to farmland as migrant laborers bought land sold by farmers and real estate agents to keep them stationary. Golden Gate Barrio was rumored to be named for the front gate of the farmhouse as it caught the sun's rays. Cuatro Milpas (four cornfields) may have been named not for the crop, but for the classic Mexican folk song.

PHOTO COURTESY ARIZONA HISTORICAL SOCIETY

This adobe structure was built by Darrell Duppa in 1870. Here it is shown in the 1940s. The building still stands today on the property of American Legion Post 41. It is considered the second oldest house in Phoenix after the Walker Jones/Alcaria Montoya house.

La Sonorita was a common barrio name across the Southwest. El Mesquital, El Campito, Green Acres and numerous others formed south of the city center. In isolation, these impoverished communities became largely self-sufficient. They built parks such as Grant Park. Enterprising Chinese businessmen opened stores, and Mexican Americans opened numerous businesses to provide for their isolated farm-working communities.

As the cotton industry exploded in the Valley, growers began importing labor to work the immense fields. Hiring agents, earning $4 a head, were sent to Mexico by the Arizona Growers Association(ACGA) to find willing labor. These *enganchadores* painted grandiose images of a good life to be found in the U.S. When combined with their experiences of the revolution ravaging their homeland, Mexicans could not refuse temptation. Between 1918 and 1921, almost 30,000 underpaid Mexican farm workers flooded into the Valley to work the growing fields and look for their salvation. What they found were dusty labor camps, low wages and severe neglect.[10]

The exploitation only worsened. There were reports of Mexican chain gangs and illegal deportation. Labor contractors were accused of bullying and abusing the workers.[11] An investigation in 1920 found that the workers were being housed in tents and overcrowded shacks with no electricity, laundry facilities, showers or water. And sometimes not even outhouses.[12]

Then in early 1921, six years after cotton had became king of industry in the Valley, the king was toppled. Boll weevils decimated cotton crops across the Southern U.S. and the market collapsed. Arizona companies went bankrupt. Cotton's dominance of Arizona's agriculture also created a disastrous side effect. When the weakened cotton harvest was done, 10,000 underfed and penniless Mexican laborers sat idle – with no other crop to harvest and no way to return home. The Mexican settlements filled to capacity and humanity began spilling over into shanty towns.[13] In the rush to import cheap Mexican labor, a social crisis had been created.

Under community pressure, the ACGA made feeble attempts to ship workers home. And though the Mexican consul in Phoenix (González Córdoba) did convince his government to send $17,000 to help the stranded population, they were largely left to fend for themselves.[14] The Mexican barrios overflowed. Their inhabitants sought any job they could find.

In time, other crops balanced the agricultural industry in Arizona, and the workers provided the labor. But by now, the barrios south of town had grown much larger, yet lost any productive connection with Phoenix proper. A dividing line between the two worlds seemed to have been etched in the minds of every Anglo citizen.

The barrios of South Phoenix were separate. In these poor tenements, Mexicans felt an inclusion, a welcome that they did not receive outside their neighborhoods. If Mexican Americans were tolerated at all in Anglo communities and businesses, it was with restrictions; such as "Mexican Day" at local swimming pools or "Mexican Night" at the Riverside Ballroom.[15]

Serving as safe havens from discrimination and segregation, the barrios grew, helped by cheap land and housing, nonexistent or weak building codes, shared language, customs, ties to family and friends, and the need for an identity with the homeland and a bridge to American society.[16]

Precursors to a movement

On a stroll, heading north from the barrios, one could watch the gradual change, approaching Washington Street. The occasional Anglo walked by as a lively downtown came into view. Continuing further on to Van Buren, "No Mexicans allowed" signs began appearing in shop windows. Still farther north, the Anglo animosity to Blacks and Mexicans was palpable on the street.

Minorities in Phoenix had nowhere to run. Unwelcome in the city proper, they also suffered deeply as the Great Depression hit. By 1933, 20 percent of Phoenix's population was unemployed, and some minorities found meager pay in labor and agriculture. There were few other options available.

There were also few organizations existing to help Latinos during this time. Even the police were of little help.

Ray Martinez would later recall the usual practices of Phoenix police:

"As an example, you know, police would stop you on the street for no reason at all. They all carried a nightstick. And they said, 'Well you just get on here, because we're having a situation here. We don't want you here. And so you better go,' and sometimes they'd give you a good whack with the nightstick and you'd go along.

"Many of the fellows were picked up. 'Cause in those days, they could pick us up, say 'investigation.' They had this thing. In other words, they could hold you about three days. In-*ves*-tigation.

"And then they could always justify it somehow or another. But one of the favorite things to do was get you in the elevator, then go up, stop the elevator between floors and beat the hell out of you – just for the hell of it."[17]

One organization that did exist was the Friendly House. But it had its issues.[18] It was started with the goal of helping teach English, find domestic work and improve the personal hygiene of immigrants. The organization also "lauded employers' efforts to deport immigrant troublemakers who sought to organize strikes. This appealed to the general population who wanted to Americanize the immigrants as a way of ensuring they conformed to Anglo-American cultural and class norms."[19]

Ray Martinez remembers his wife's story of employment through the Friendly House:

> "My wife – just out of grammar school – went to the Friendly House, you know to hire out. ... She was sent to a lawyer and his wife. They were just moving into an apartment. Well, they told her it'd be about a week's work. And she'd be paid 10 dollars.
>
> "Well ... Seven days she worked. And I mean 8 to 10 hours a day. And, then of course, in those days, too, they hired young Hispanic girls ... Why? An effort was made, you know – sexual harassment. And they had to suffer those indignities too, you know – when the wife wasn't home.
>
> " ... So, at the end ... my wife said when she was through, she asked the lady, 'I'm through. You don't need me so ...'And the wife called out to the husband, said, 'Honey, give me the 10 dollars so I can pay.'
>
> "I already paid her."[20]

But Friendly House, Mexicans and Mexican Americans all faced a bigger problem.

As the U.S. Depression-era economy struggled, Americanization gave way to the idea of repatriation. Barely 10 years had passed since Mexico's revolution sparked an enormous exodus of refugees to the U.S. In the decade following Mexican President Venustiano Carranza's death in 1920, Mexico would struggle through the Cristero Rebellion and numerous attempts to overtake an unstable government.

As the 1930s began, Mexican officials were still flush with the ideas their revolution had promised. But the country was depleted of its population. To bring citizens home, they promised cheap land, cooperative farming communities and other benefits if citizens would return. But as half a million Mexican nationals crossed the border, the government in Mexico City found itself ill-prepared to keep its promises, leaving its citizens stranded at the international border waiting to return for better economic times in the U.S.[21]

Early Latino organizations in Phoenix

Alianza Hispano-Americano
Founded in Tucson, 1894
Joined forces in 1920 with Phoenix Americanization Committee to form Friendly House.

La Liga Protectora
Founded in Phoenix, 1915 - 1930s
Pedro Garcia de la Lama formed La Liga to fight a proposed law that limited the number of Mexican Americans a company could hire.

League of United Latin American Citizens (LULAC)
Founded in Corpus Christi, Texas 1929 - present
The oldest existing Hispanic civil rights organization in U.S.

The Latino American Club
Founded in Phoenix, AZ 1933 - 1950s
Its goal was to educatate Mexican Americans in politics and find work during the Great Depression.

La Sociedad Mutualista Porfirio Diaz
Founded 1907 - 1950s Provided insurance to Latinos who could not get it otherwise.

The U.S. had begun a repatriation program as early as 1928. In 1929, President Herbert Hoover opened the floodgates by authorizing the Mexican repatriation program. By the end of 1931, roads in Texas were choked with Mexicans and Mexican Americans going to Mexico. Trains in California were loaded with Latinos, regardless of their legality in the U.S. Locally, Placida Garcia Smith – the new director of Friendly House – attempted to help families repatriate from the Valley. She, too, had been blinded by the empty promises of Mexican consulates in Phoenix. The Great Depression wore on.

During this tragic program, more than a half million Mexicans and Mexican Americans were sent back to Mexico. In 1933, Garcia Smith would report having helped 130 families to the border since the previous spring. The following year, with the election of President Franklin D. Roosevelt and his promised New Deal, repatriation began to slowly fade as new solutions to the Great Depression were sought.[22]

One future Post 41 member, Valdemar Córdova, would watch as his father, Luis, became frustrated with the unconstitutional madness of the repatriation. In 1932, Luis founded the Latino American Club, another organization to help Latinos during the 1930s that would be more political than Friendly House – and possibly form some of the roots of Post 41's political activism years later.

Luis Hernandez Córdova was a boilermaker for the Southern Pacific

Placida Garcia Smith

Placida Garcia Smith was born in 1896 in the town her Mexican grandfather founded, Conejos, Colo. Her father was the town sheriff and the men he dragged into his jail cells invoked empathy in Placida for society's problems.

After graduating high school in 1915, she attended universities in Colorado, California, Utah and Mexico.

In 1929 she came to Phoenix when her husband, Reginal, landed a job at the Arizona Republic.

Placida became director of Friendly House in May 1931.

Seven years later her husband died.

The young widow poured her heart into Friendly House, teaching English classes and helping people of all nationalities gain their citizenship.

In the 1940s, gentle, soft-spoken Placida spoke out on slum clearance and joined numerous committees and boards.

In 1949, she would asist Adam Diaz in bringing an exhibition baseball game to Phoenix between the New York Giants and Mexican All-Stars of Sonora. Extra activities were run by Ray Martinez of Post 41.

In 1950 she was sent as an official U.S. Representative at the inauguration of Mexican President Miguel Aleman.

By 1960, she had received honors from the Daughters of the American Revolution

and from Las Damas del Valle.

In September 1960, Placida's beloved Friendly House moved into a larger building. Post 41 offered a portion of its property to be used for parking.

In 1961, she was named Phoenix Woman of the Year in a ceremony at the Westward Ho.

When she stepped down as director in 1963, she had helped more than 1,000 people gain their citizenship. She continued teaching until 1970.

Placida passed away in July 1981.

Railroad and long known as a leader of the Mexican American community. Though his Latino American Club's focus was political, it was also a safe haven for Latinos as jobs became scarce and the tragedy of Mexican repatriation began.

Throughout the decade, several chapters of the Latino American Club would form across Arizona. They convened in Phoenix with hopes of increasing Latino involvement in the political system. They often endorsed candidates appealing to Mexican Americans, such as Tucsonan Conrad James Carreón, a slender man wiho gave explosive speeches and would represent Phoenix as the first Spanish-speaking representative in the Arizona State Legislature in 1938. His political career would span 25 years.

Politicians were invited to meet with the club and discuss the community's needs, and the club sought to increase voting power by organizing drives and rallies across southern Arizona.[23]

Such political activism would inspire a future generation to become involved. As a young man, Phoenix's first Hispanic city council member – Adam Diaz – found himself involved in these drives, going "house to house, door to door (to) explain to people" what they were trying to do.[24]

> **"The most serious threat to our unity and way of life is the greatest of all enemies within, INTOLERANCE, whose most ugly phase is racial and religious bigotry. ... I shall use the full power of my office to smite the ugly head of intolerance whenever and wherever it may appear."**
>
> – Conrad James "Jimmie" Carreon in a statement that he would run for Congress in 1942

Unfortunately, the Latino American Club was not immune to weaknesses. In 1935, the club asked the Phoenix City Commission to exclude Blacks from using Southside Park on 2nd Avenue and Grant Street, in a largely Mexican community.[25]

To further complicate life, the Latino American Club would be one of many organizations that could not meet the challenges of hard survival in the Great Depression. Nor, for all its successes, was the club able to change the second-class status of Latinos' lives in Arizona.

Luis' son, Valdemar, would later recall the continued exclusion of Latinos:

> "Here in Phoenix, up to World War II, we could not live where we wanted to. In some areas they would not rent or sell to a Mexican American. At the Fox Theatre, you had to sit upstairs. At the Studio Theatre in downtown Phoenix, you couldn't even get in. At the public parks, such as University Park – which was founded and maintained with city tax dollars which we all paid – a Mexican American was not permitted."[26]

As Roosevelt's New Deal took hold, and his "Good Neighbor Policy" with Latin American countries helped improve difficult relations, Mexican Americans still found life hard in the U.S. But there was one organization offering an escape. It could provide jobs, a place to sleep and food to eat: the military.

A history in battle

"This is a fight between a free world and a slave world."
– Vice President Henry A. Wallace, May 8, 1942

On Jan. 3, 1939, just before World War II ignited, David Perez walked into the Arizona Army National Guard office to enlist. At 17, he was still a gangly high school student who was leaving behind his job at a local aluminum company to step into a U.S. Army uniform.

In a 2003 interview, he recalled with a light-hearted laugh, what had brought him there. "In 1938 ... I went to enlist in the daytime. They say 'well right now we don't have openings for Mexicans. But there's gonna be two openings January the 1st of 1939. So on January 3rd – it was drill night – I went and sure enough there was a vacancy. So that's when I joined."[27]

Perez's enlistment was anything but new. A long thread of Latinos in U.S. military history can be traced to the American Revolution when Louisiana Territorial Governor Bernardo de Gálvez y Madrid with his 1,400 Spanish troops battled the British across the coastal waters of the Atlantic and the Gulf of Mexico. His efforts would aid the American Colonies in their battle for independence.

When the Civil War began in 1861, more than 3,000 Mexican Americans enlisted on both sides. By war's end, that number had grown to 10,000. In 1864, Rear Admiral David Glasgow Farragut and his fleet pushed into Mobile Bay upon his famous command, "Damn the torpedoes." The crew successfully captured the Confederate Navy's CSS Tennessee, and Farragut became the U.S. Navy's first full admiral.

At the turn of the 20th century, Theodore Roosevelt's "Rough Riders" would fight on Cuban soil in the Spanish-American War. Captain Maximiliano Luna of New Mexico would serve with distinction, and George Armijo would go on to serve as a U.S. Congressman. Many Hispanic members of the Arizona National Guard would also join Roosevelt's volunteer cavalry regiment.

Two years later, during the Boxer Rebellion in China, Pvt. France Silva of the U.S. Marines became the first Mexican American to earn a Medal of Honor for attempting to defend the Tartar Walls that surrounded Beijing and rebuild a barricade. Several men had already been killed in the battle. Yet, when a bullet ripped through Silva's elbow and ricocheted off his chest leaving a vicious wound, he refused to step back to safety. Despite only being able to hold a small pistol, he continued to relieve guards through the next day. The following year he was awarded the medal while stationed on Mare Island.

David Glasgow
Farragut

In 1916, the Latino military legacy grew as the largely Mexican American 1st Arizona Infantry followed Col. A.M. Tuthill and Gen. John J. Pershing into Mexico in a year-long pursuit of Pancho Villa, who had raided Columbus, N.M., and killed 17 Americans. Two months after the troops withdrew from Mexico they were mobilized for World War I on April 6, 1917.

Across the nation, some 200,000 Latinos would be enlisted to fight in World War I. Most were Mexican American, with 18,000 Puerto Ricans joining their ranks. In Arizona, more than 12,000 men would be drafted or enlisted, such as Frank Valenzuela, whose family had homesteaded in Arizona since 1877.

Latinos still felt the heat of discrimination in the military. They were often drafted as "buck privates" – soldiers at the lowest grade of the lowest rank – not even receiving a stripe on their shoulder. Soldiers who could not speak English well were sent to language training centers and integrated into the mainstream army, often given menial tasks.

David Barkley Cantú was one of just two Mexican Americans who gained recognition for their service in World War I. Cantú received the Medal of Honor posthumously, having died in the Meuse River after completing an essential scouting mission in November 1918. It wasn't discovered until years later that indeed he was Latino. He had used his Anglo father's surname, Barkley, to avoid being segregated out of the front lines.[28]

Marcelino Serna, circa 1920s

The other soldier, Marcelino Serna, received the Distinguished Service Cross and the French Croix de Guerre for his Herculean feat in Meuse-Argonne, France, on Sept. 12, 1918.

Serna had come to the U.S. two years earlier in search of work on the railroads and in the sugarbeet fields of Colorado. Now he was a sharpshooting private with B Company of the 355th infantry, 89th Division.

Trailing the sniper he had wounded, he came across a German bunker, killed 26, and facilitated the capture of another 24 Germans. And this was after a similar feat at St. Mihiel where he killed six and captured eight Germans.

He related the experience to an *El Paso Times* reporter in 1962.

"I jumped up and ran about ten yards and then hit the dirt. I kept this up until I was in the machine gunner's left flank. He had hit my helmet twice with bullets during this run.

"When I got close enough, I threw four grenades into the nest. Eight Germans came out with their hands up. Another six were in the nest dead. I held my prisoners until help arrived."

Six days before the Armistice Serna was shot in the leg by a sniper, and hobbled back to safety.

On June 19, 1919, Germany signed the Treaty of Versailles, and World War I came to an end. That same year, U.S. relations with Japan were growing shaky, and the beginnings of War Plan Orange were formed in preparation for the possibility of a conflict with the ambitious island nation. Some feared it was just a matter of time before the two nations clashed.

In September 1919, a young Adolf Hitler was sent to investigate the German Workers Party – a suspicious group meeting with Marxist ideals of which Germany disapproved. Instead, Hitler became interested in the movement, starting a political trajectory that would change the world. The stage was being set for World War II, a global conflict that would see 16.1 million U.S. military personnel deployed in the Allied fight.

This was the history into which young David Perez and the founding members of Post 41 would step.

1940s

'Air raid Pearl Harbor. This is not drill.'

Nine months passed between David Perez's enlistment and Pearl Harbor's fateful day. During that time, the world began its spiral into World War II. On Sept. 1, 1939, Poland was overrun by 1.8 million German troops. Two days later Great Britain, France, Australia and New Zealand would declare war against Germany.

Life did not change drastically for Phoenix or much of the U.S. over the next two years. But the U.S. government wasn't about to relax. As the possibility of war neared, American troops were shuffled around the globe and trained to their specific tasks.

In 1940, two national guard units from New Mexico were mobilized: the 200th and the 515th Coast Artillery (anti-aircraft). Many of these men were Latinos from New Mexico, Arizona and Texas – often selected, in part, because they spoke Spanish – one of two official languages in the country where they would be stationed, the Philippines.[1] Their new home was to be Clark Field, 65 miles from the capital of Manila.

On Sept. 16, 1940, the Arizona National Guard mobilized its famous troops, now named the 158th Infantry Regiment. In February 1941, after training at Fort Sill, Okla., the 158th was sent to Camp Barkley, Texas, and then on to Louisiana.[2]

Most Mexican Americans felt a deeply patriotic calling. Young Ray Martinez was determined to enlist in the armed forces, but nobody would accept him. Army, Marines, Air Force; they all turned him down. Their reason was a metal plate in his left arm. At 15, Ray had been struck by a car while delivering newspapers. But something was about to happen that would change recruiters' minds.[3]

In the midst of the holiday season, in the dark morning hours on six Japanese aircraft carriers, planes were taking off for the Hawaiian island of Oahu and into American infamy. It was December 7th, 1941.

Hours later, Joe Torres was shining his shoes when suddenly people began yelling in the streets. He looked up to see their faces as they called out, "Pearl Harbor's been bombed!"

Sgt. David Perez was downtown at a movie in Texas when a voice interrupted to call out, "All military personnel report to your units. Pearl Harbor has been bombed."

Steve Zozaya was sick, laid up in the hospital. "I was having a good time ... no training. Not getting up in the morning. So when we heard, when the announcement came that Pearl Harbor had been bombed; one day that hospital was full of troops. But the next day that hospital was empty. Everybody wanted out."[3]

Pete Dimas was in his parents' car with friends when he turned the radio on and heard the announcement. After the news report, he turned to the others, "We're going. We have to get it and we have to go."[4]

Four days later, Germany and Italy declared war on the U.S. and so began this country's participation in World War II. Within six months, Ray took a test for enlistment in the Navy. He had finally been accepted into the armed forces.

Bataan and Corregidor

Nine hours after Pearl Harbor was attacked, Clark Field was hit. Personnel knew about the surprise attack in Hawaii 30 minutes after it had begun, but still were caught off guard. The 515th and 200th Coast Artillery regiments were never told of an impending attack on their own base. They had spent three peaceful months enjoying the theater that had been set up, taking day trips to Manila and fighting boredom.

That morning, planes took off from Clark Field and headed north to spot any Japanese bombers that might be headed their way. When nothing was seen, they returned to base and headed for the mess hall to fill their empty stomachs. As the pilots sat down to eat, the sky filled with Japanese

1940s-era map illustrating the layout of the early battle in the Philippines.

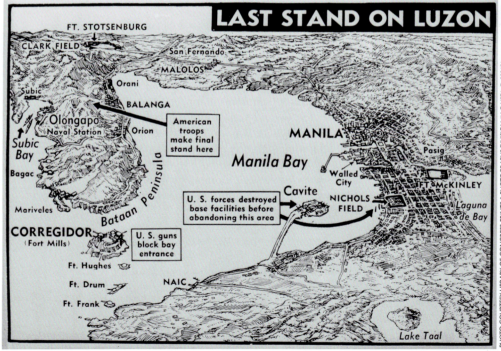

planes flying too high to hit with the base guns. As the bombs fell, smaller plans swooped in to strafe what remained. The pilots' mess hall tent fell quiet, with Epimenio Rubi of Winslow among the first American casualties in the Philippines.

Two more fields were attacked throughout the Philippines – Iba Field in Zambales and Nichols Field near Manila. Troops fell back into the walled city of Manila as it came under siege. Then the headquarters of the U.S. Asiatic Fleet at Cavite was struck. Two days later, Japan began to move ground troops in on the overwhelmed U.S. and Philippine troops.

For two weeks, the American forces struggled to maintain a foothold in the Philippines. Realizing the insanity of staying put, Gen. Douglas MacArthur pulled back his troops into the Bataan Peninsula, west of Manila. From there, they moved to a fortified island, Corregidor. It was an embattled retreat. The Japanese pushed through three separate lines of defense as U.S. and Philippine forces struggled to hold ground. On March 12, Gen. MacArthur, his family and staff boarded four PT boats and sped to Mindanao, then to Australia. On April 3 the Japanese rained down artillery on the defending forces. It took them three days to punch through the struggling defenses.

The troops fell back again – starving, surrounded, trapped. They could last only so long.

PHOTO COURTESY OF THE CHICANO COLLECTION, DEPARTMENT OF ARCHIVES AND SPECIAL COLLECTIONS, ARIZONA STATE UNIVERSITY

Seaman Ray Martinez joins the USS Makkassar Strait as a radio man.

Father Albert Braun

On the morning of April 9, 1942, U.S. and Filipino forces on the Bataan peninsula surrendered. Corregidor Island was the only stronghold left. That day, a thin voice called out from a radio broadcast, the "Voice of Freedom," deep in Corregidor's Malinta Tunnel:

"Bataan has fallen. The Philippine-American troops on this war-ravaged and bloodstained peninsula have laid down their arms. With heads bloody but unbowed, they have yielded to the superior force and numbers of the enemy.

"The world will long remember the epic struggle that Filipino and American soldiers put up in the jungle fastness and along the rugged coast of Bataan. They have stood up uncomplaining under the constant and grueling fire of the enemy for more than three months. Besieged on land and blockaded by sea, cut off from all sources of help in the Philippines and in America, the intrepid fighters have done all that human endurance could bear."

Corregidor was all the soldiers had left. The island was two miles from shore, yet honeycombed with tunnels and armed with mortar batteries high enough to shoot beyond its lower hills. There on its rocks stood Fathers Albert Braun and Herman Baumann. It was close enough to watch the mainland and see captured soldiers filing ghostlike through the trees under the watchful guns of their Japanese captors.

The prisoners would walk for 12 days, over 85 miles of jungle and

PHOTO COURTESY FRANK BARRIOS

Albert Braun as a young chaplain during World War I. Despite wounds received on the battlefield, Braun remained through the day and night, ministering to the wounded men and giving last rites to the dead. For his efforts, he would receive the Purple Heart and the Distinguished Service Cross and the Silver Star.

underbrush, dying as they went. The Bataan Death March had begun. A large number of the troops killed or captured were Mexican Americans, intensifying the fervor of U.S. Latinos during the war.[5]

As they marched on, Braun and Baumann waited with their fellow troops on Corregidor. They stayed in the open with their soldiers even as the island siege began. They only descended into the caves when needed for rites at a makeshift hospital in the bowels of the mountain.

Each night, from partially-repaired antennas, the "Voice of Freedom" radio broadcast out of Corregidor's Malinta Tunnel then signed off with the defiant words, "Corregidor still stands!"

Two hundred feet below Malinta Hill at the island's center, they felt nervously safe. The soldiers fought on through a daily barrage of artillery from the Japanese. But as they suffered under the bombs, Gen. Jonathan Wainwright realized could not let the enemy reach Malinta Tunnel in battle – there were too many wounded and defenseless men there. Over the radio, he offered to surrender the island.

A month after Bataan had been overrun, Corregidor fell on May 7.

The soldiers were in a painful state. A month pinned in the tunnels had forced all of life to take place there. The stench of excrement and rotting bodies overpowered everyone. Their Japanese captors refused permission to bury the dead, who had begun to decompose. Others tried, but it was Braun who found some way to secure the opportunity to perform rites. The bodies were necessarily burned, and the bones buried.

He celebrated Mass with the makeshift hospital's wounded soldiers at the mouth of the tunnel, though he was not permitted access to the soldiers at the bottom-side garage area. Instead, he would slip through Japanese troops as a litter-bearer and give what services he could without detection.

In July, Braun found himself and others shipped to Bilibid prison in Manila, then to Cabanatuan prison in central Luzon, and numerous other prisons. In each, the priest would scrape together survival with determination and stolen scraps of food, while ministering to fellow prisoners.

Western tears

As the Asian continent boiled with warfare, other Arizona Latinos fought in some of Europe's most heart-breaking battles. Back home, still more of Arizona's eager men and women set aside their lives and poured into the recruiting offices and shipped off to fight on numerous fronts.

Luis Córdova's son, Valdemar put life on hold to join the military at 18, before he had even finished high school. He was two classes shy of graduating from Phoenix Union High School and left behind a hard-earned reputation as a basketball star and put on hold feelings he had for a young girl, Gloria.

With his training complete, the young man shipped out to England in late 1943. He joined the 8th Air Force at Edge of Ipswich, 60 miles outside of London. Early the following year, he had successfully completed 14 missions in a B-17 bomber over targets in Germany.

The 15th trip would be different.

Second Lt. Córdova's plane droned over Germany as anti-aircraft shells began to fly. It was Jan. 29, 1944, when enemy fire tore through their B-17 above Frankfurt, Germany. The crew bailed out of the plummeting B-17, and parachuted to safety. But Córdova was captured.

The Stalag Luft 1 Berth Prisoner of War camp would become home for the next year and a half. He was listed as a POW by the U.S. War Dept. in April 1944, along with fellow Arizonan and flyboy Sgt. Frank G. Mabante of the 525th.

Córdova would receive the Purple Heart.[6]

The beaches of Normandy

For the first three years, the war against Germany was fought from the eastern side. Then a plan was made for the Allies to squeeze Germany from the other side. It would start with an assault onto the beaches in southern France, Operation Neptune. Never before or since has so large an invasion taken place in one day. Approximately 140,000 troops were to step onto Normandy's beaches on Tuesday morning, June 6, 1944.

It was the night after a full moon as the ships moved in. The tide dropped and the men approached. At 6:30 a.m., as the sky began to brighten, the first ground troops made their move onto the beach at Omaha. The invasion of Normandy had begun.

The events of the day were so much more than Pvt. 1st Class Philip Fierros could have anticipated.

Hunched over on a landing cruiser with the other men, he waited. "I don't remember what time it was. But It was pretty rough. ... Well, we uh ... was a bunch of us, was a full load in one of these ... *como se llamen?* ... Yeah, those flat jobs. We were all packed in one of those things with all your pack and everything and your duffle bag. And I thought well, as soon as we get off we're here to camp or something.

"No. From then on it was go, go."

More than 10,000 Allied soldiers

Troops in an LCVP landing craft approaching "Omaha" Beach on "D-Day", June 6, 1944

PHOTO ARMY SIGNAL CORPS COLLECTION IN U.S. NATIONAL ARCHIVES.

would die in that invasion. Another 4,000 to 9,000 German soldiers would lose their lives. Young Fierros would survive that fateful day and battle his way across France and into Germany. After the war, he would receive a Silver Service Star and two Purple Hearts for his contribution.[7]

Two days after the initial landing at Normandy, another Phoenician from the barrios would step into the destruction of Normandy's beaches.

Miguel Gomez had met his high school sweetheart, Dora Mendoza, at a street dance in the park. She was a fast-pitch softball player who caught his fancy. They married soon after high school. By May 1943, Miguel was working as a stock boy at a clothing store in Phoenix and Dora was expecting their first child.

Then the government called for young Miguel. Before being sent off to boot camp, he paid $20 to change his name from Miguel to Mike. Perhaps he was worried about the discrimination and ridicule heaped on Latino soldiers during World War I. But in the end, with bullets in the air and men dying, it ultimately didn't matter where a soldier came from. What did matter was risking one's life for a fellow soldier.

His two brothers would also be drafted.

"The United States drafted 18- and 19-year-olds because younger men do not feel fear to the depth that men in their mid-20's do," Gomez recalled in an interview. "Younger men feel invincible, and the seriousness of the situation does not completely register with the young soldiers."[8]

The soldiers were young, but fear was still there. It could be seen in the cigarettes they constantly held to their lips and the prayers that were spoken without privacy. Gomez remembers these moments clearly as he approached a beach in Normandy.

On June 8, 1944, the D-Day invasion was in its third day. Hundreds of ships approached in the latest wave by the 837th Ordinance Combat Depot Company of Gen. Patton's 3rd Army. Mike Gomez waited on one ship, his 19-year old body braced for the coming battle. He was praying aloud.[9]

The men descended ropes and stepped into landing craft that would cross the shallow churning waters to the shore. A thousand or more floating bodies tossed in the waves as the men drew closer.

Gomez remembered later, "We ran like hell when we got to the beaches. It's a matter of survival, but you always have a little fear in you. It's their life or yours." Then, a surreal moment touched him in the whirlwind.

As mortars and bullets showered the beachheads, Gomez jumped into a crater left by an exploding shell. There with him was another soldier from a different unit – Frank Calles. They had lived nearby in the barrios back home and became friends. Imagine the surprise of meeting a friend from the barrio on the battlefield 5,000 miles from home. Yet here they were, with a moment to reflect on the chance encounter, so many miles and an ocean away from home. But only for a moment.

They each burst out into the open and dashed for the next place of cover. Frank Calles disappeared into the madness. Both would survive, but years would pass before they reunited again, back in Phoenix.

For the moment, there was still a war to fight.

Desperate days

By June 1942, Pete G. Dimas had enlisted, just as he had promised the day he heard on a car radio that Pearl Harbor had been bombed. After training, he was assigned to the 106th Infantry and sent to a peaceful front line near Luxembourg, in the thick, forested hills of the Ardennes Mountains.

Dimas would be made Army cook, thanks to experience in the Civilian Conservation Corps as a "dog robber," serving meals to officers, clearning their quarters and making their beds. Now, standing over the stark Army meals, he daydreamed about his mother's cooking back home. Sopapillas, chili with carne sauce. The most delicious beans.

As the December air froze Europe in 1944, Hitler's army was still reeling from the surprise attack on the beaches of Normandy, France. He and his generals began planning a secret offensive to split the Allied front line in Ardennes and circle back on the weakened forces. It was to be Germany's last bold success of the war.

The predawn silence of Dec. 16 shattered as German artillery pummeled the front lines. The Battle of the Bulge had begun. Two days later, Pete Dimas' division, near the town of Bastogne, struggled to hold its line.

Dimas, one of Post 41's first members, remembers the battle well in a striking 2004 interview. The true pain of what he saw comes through; his eyes showing none of his years, yet all of the sorrow as the viewer is pulled back to that day, told not by an Allied soldier, but by a man whose friends died at his side.

" ... We looked beyond. I forgot what direction. And Bastogne was on fire. You could see the flame. The red fire, you know, the reflection.

"They'd shoot artillery for a little while. And they stopped altogether. Then the German rifleman was coming, and they were making a lot of noise. They do that. Make you feel worse. They were hollering, and they were coming and they start shooting machine guns. And we start seeing them and we start shooting back, you know?

"We were holed there for about ... I don't know what it was, 20 minutes or a half hour. But it seems to me it was a long time. And the men were getting wounded, getting shot. And we stayed there until the captain gave the order. 'Men we can't ... we are losing too many men here. We just have to pull out. We have to, you know ... retreat.'"

In the interview Sgt. Dimas' voice goes soft, lost in the memory.

"And we had to retreat. And I could see the men getting, you know ... wounded pretty *badly*. And it seems like when you're in that condition to me ..."

Dimas is overcome by the memories. He looks down, his jaw line shakes as if he can still feel that cold winter. "That the men were getting ..." he pauses again, the words painfull on his lips. Clearing his

Pete Dimas with his wife, Beatrice

throat he continues, " ... shot, getting killed. Hurt me."

Dimas' hand gestures in frustration with the emotion. "We were so close together, you know?" He looks down with the innocent, powerless sorrow of a young man. The moment is over and one is left with somber respect for the soldier's world.

Three days after the battle began, despite constant maneuvering and robbed of energy by skirmishes in the snow drifts and bogs of the Ardennes, Sgt. Dimas and the few men left of his unit were captured. Dimas was one of the last to surrender.

The German soldiers permitted Dimas and another soldier to build a stretcher out of branches and an overcoat to carry one wounded friend up to a nearby road where the Red Cross would pick him up. The two men turned away from the road, hands on their heads, and rejoined their captured troops.

During the night the prisoners marched through a city that had been decimated. They sang "God Bless America" as they passed the ruins. "We kept on singing and singing and singing and singing. And walking and walking, and we just wanted to let the Germans know that we weren't licked yet," Dimas said.[10]

When the Battle of the Bulge was lost, more than 7,000 Americans became prisoners in World War II's largest mass surrender of U.S. troops in the European Theater.

For three months, Dimas was listed as missing in action. Then, in early 1945, a letter found its way to his family.

Dimas had been taken to Prison Camp Stalag 4B Muhlberg Sachsen 51-13, near the Czechoslovakian border. It was an enormous prison filled with emaciated soldiers made worse by over-crowding. It was the same internment camp that author Kurt Vonnegut Jr. would write about in his 1969 novel "Slaughterhouse-Five."

In Dimas' own words, he wrote home, "So far I am getting enough to eat and I have a place to sleep. As soon as the war is over with Germany, I will come home. So let's make the best of it and hope it won't be long."

The reality may not have been so simple. He would remember in later interviews that he "saw quite a few people that died while I was a prisoner."[11] He recalled one prisoner being shot in the head simply because he had become too sick to move.

But Dimas survived. The threat of starvation was held back with a loaf of bread for every seven men and the occasional cup of fetid soup, alive with worms – forcing the men to pick them out before eating.

Then his luck changed. Four months after his capture, the Russians were advancing on the scattering Germans at the Elbe River. As the Nazi troops fled, U.S. soldiers came across the river in a canoe to rescue the prisoners of war. Dimas was among those rescued in April, 1945, and flown to France on a C-47 cargo plane.

"You could hardly believe it when you were liberated. I was jumping up and down even though I felt sick."[12]

In 1969, Kurt Vonnegut would write a story drawing on his experiences in the same POW camp that Sgt. Pete Dimas saw. *Slaughterhouse-Five* has become known as an American classic anti-war, science fiction novel.

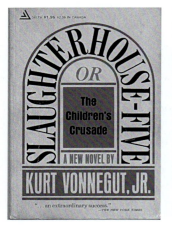

Along a wooded road

Silvestre Santana Herrera's story may be the best known of Latino heroes in World War II. It was another example of will and putting your unit before yourself. And it made Herrera one of the most celebrated Hispanic soldiers in Arizona.

Rain soaked into their clothes as the soldiers filed along a quiet forest road in northern France. Silvestre Herrera and his platoon were advancing along the dirt road as it cut through the dark trees of a forest near the village of Mertzwiller, close to the German border. It was the morning of March 15, 1945. Allied forces had taken the Rhine. They were on the verge of victory against Germany. Pfc. Herrera was an acting squad leader/automatic rifleman. Company E 142nd Infantry of the 36th (Texas) Infantry Division was the lead element as it moved into German-held territory.

His best friend was a sergeant he had nicknamed "Squirrelly." Herrera would later honor his friend by giving his grandson the same nickname. But today, he was alone in his thoughts, scouting ahead 400 yards from his companions, his M1 rifle close and ready.

What was he doing here? Months before, he was with his expectant wife and three children. Murky events surround the days after he received his draft notice in 1944. The generally accepted story is as follows:

He had grown up in El Paso under the watchful eyes of Librado and Gertrudis Santana. With them, he worked in the crop fields. In 1927, he traveled to Phoenix with Librado to work at local farms and at a dairy. Along the way he would meet Ramona Hidalgo Guerrera. They married in 1939 and three children soon followed: Mary, Elva and Silvestre Jr. A fourth baby was waiting to enter the world when Silvestre received his draft notice. He was 27.[13]

What he didn't know is that Librado and Gertrudis were not his parents. His father was really an uncle who had brought 1-year-old Silvestre to El Paso when his parents died in the 1918 influenza pandemic in Silvestre's hometown of Ciudad Camargo, Chihuahua, Mexico. The discovery was made when Librado told him, exclaiming, "You don't have to go, you're not American."

But Silvestre couldn't see sending somebody else to fight in his place. He may have been Mexican, but he had lived in the U.S. most of his life. His family was there. His friends were there.

And so it was. Herrera reported for boot camp at Fort McClellan, Ala. He was assigned to the Texas Army National Guard. Soon he was shipping out with the first American unit to land in Europe during World War II.

That seemed like such a long time ago. Herrera now had the present on which to focus. He and the other soldiers continued along that road.

Then the quiet air was pierced.

Gunfire blasted from the trees. Two German machine gun posts sent some of the platoon diving for cover. Others dropped to the dirt road and crouched along the edge. In the commotion, Herrera was unable to tell where orders were coming from. He shouted and sprang up to move forward.

Spotting the barrel flash of a machine gun in the trees, he leveled his own weapon to fire back as he ran forward. He dropped three German soldiers with his bullets. When he was close enough, he hurled a hand grenade at the emplacement. Then another.

Before anybody had time to think, eight Germans had surrendered.

Decades later, Herrera would remember, "Those Germans, they were really nice people. I remember they all had bad trench foot when we captured them.[14]

"I remember I kept thinking to myself that I had to do everything I could to give my company a chance to advance, and so, that's what I did. There was too much at stake."

As his unit took control of its prisoners, Herrera crawled ahead, bullets ripping through the air from a second machine gun. Herrera continued to fire rounds in hopes of keeping the enemy pinned so his platoon could advance. As the platoon crept forward, it was stopped by increased machine gun fire and a minefield.

Some of the men threw rocks into the field, attempting to trigger the mines and make passage safe. Again, Herrera pushed ahead of the others with his own technique. "I knew there was a minefield. I had a two-by-four and was pushing it ahead of me," he explained in a later interview. Then impatience got the best of him.

He tossed aside the board, and "that's when I made my mistake."[15]

Silvestre stepped on a landmine. When he came back down to the ground, he hit yet another.

He looked down to see his boots were gone, and his pant legs on fire. In those two moments, he had lost both feet and part of one leg just below the knee.

He reached for his rifle.

Herrera somehow clutched at his M-1 Garand rifle and lifted it to the trees. He applied a bandage to his leg and dragged his body to the rocks.

Silvestre Herrera in 1946. After the war, Herrera would make a living as a leather worker and silversmith.

PHOTO COURTESY OF AMERICAN LEGION POST 41

He braced himself and began firing at the enemy. He hit at least one of the Germans and forced the others to stop shooting and take cover.

Under Herrera's covering fire, his platoon moved in and killed the German machine gun crew. The platoon found a path through the minefield and located a bleeding and injured Herrera. They rushed him back to an aid station. Later, Herrera was sent to an Army hospital in Utah.[16]

The next day, the Americans began a massive artillery barrage and the 142nd forded the Zintzel River at the small village of Mertzwiller. In one week, they had stepped on German soil. On May 7, Germany surrendered.

Finally back in the states, Herrera was still coming to terms with his new life. He looked up from a slice of watermelon to see a face in the shade of the Chinaberry tree. A telegram had been delivered to him. He was needed in Washington. The president was going to honor him.

He was decorated by President Truman on the afternoon of Aug. 23, 1945, at the White House. That day, bending down to drape the medal around Herrera's neck, the president spoke quietly, "I would rather be awarded the Medal of Honor than be president of the United States."[17]

Herrera flashed that infectious smile as those words made him even prouder.

During the ceremony, twenty seven soldiers were awarded the Medal of Honor, more than any other time before in U.S. history. In March 1946, Herrera was discharged from the Army as a sergeant and a hero.

The official record reads as follows:

> *He advanced with the platoon along a wooded road until stopped by heavy enemy machinegun fire. As the rest of the unit took cover, he made a 1-man frontal assault on a strongpoint and captured 8 enemy soldiers. When the platoon resumed its advance and was subjected to fire from a 2nd emplacement beyond an extensive minefield, Prvt. 1st class Herrera again moved forward disregarding the danger of exploding mines, to attack the position. He stepped on a mine and had both feet severed but, despite intense pain and unchecked blood loss, he pinned down the enemy with accurate rifle fire while a friendly squad captured the enemy gun skirting the minefield and rushing in from the flank. The magnificent courage, extraordinary heroism, and willing self-sacrifice displayed by Pvt. Herrera resulted in the capture of 2 enemy strongpoints and the taking of 8 prisoners.*

No greater fighting team

After the attack on Pearl Harbor pulled the U.S. into war, more Hispanics than ever were would enlist in the armed forces. The decimation on Bataan Peninsula had touched many of their lives, with the largely Latino troops of the 200th and 515th trapped by the Japanese.

But earlier in September 1940, Col. J. Prugh Herndon of Tucson had already formed a group of men to train for jungle warfare. He chose the 158th Battalion of Arizona. They were mobilized in anticipation of hostilities and sent to Fort Sill, Okla., and then in February of 1941 to Camp Barkeley, Texas. As hostilities erupted, the men were shipped yet again. This time to Panama.

The Panama Canal was a key location and of interest to both the Japanese and the Germans. Six days after Christmas, the 158th Infantry Regiment shipped out to train for a year and two months in the Central American jungles and to provide a military presence in what was seen as a risk zone – the vital thread between the Atlantic and Pacific oceans.

Here they earned a new nickname. David Perez chuckles as he recalls the way it came about.

"They decided to have a bet between the 5th and the 158th: race across the isthmus – which is about 50 miles from one coast to the other ... but with a heck of a mountain range you have to go through. So, being that we were strangers to

the jungle, they thought we'd be whipped. But we fooled 'em. Hehe! The 158th got there before the 5th. And along the way there, I guess they picked the Bushmasters from the snake that is very common there in the jungle. It's a very aggressive snake. And it's more or less a night feeder, and it doesn't give you much time to pray, before you're gone.[8]

A patch was designed. It was blue and white with a snake coiled around a machete.

But while the Bushmasters were winning bets by hacking through a jungle in Central America, the embattled men on Bataan Peninsula continued to struggle for survival. They could not last. As he retreated, Gen. MacArthur turned to declare, "I came out of Bataan, and I shall return." MacArthur needed men capable of helping him keep his promise. He needed the Bushmasters.

In early 1943, the Bushmasters stepped out of the Central American jungles and onto converted passenger ocean liners bound for Brisbane, Australia. For two years, they had trained as an efficient unit with the capacity as independent soldiers capable of commando-style jungle combat. But it would be months before they engaged in battle.

At the end of December 1943, it was finally decided to test the skills of the 158th on embattled Arawe Peninsula. Two months later, in February 1944, they finally succeeded in that first grueling battle. Back home, Gov. Sidney P. Osborn honored them by proclaiming Jan. 28 Bushmasters Day.

Rested up, the 158th would battle for the airfield on Wakde Island off the north coast of Dutch New Guinea. Forty lives would be lost over three days. Advancing forward to the Sarmi region of mainland New Guinea would cost them another 400 soldiers. They lost 45 men on the Batangas Peninsula, March 12, 1945. They invaded the Bicol Peninsula of southern Luzon and the city of Legaspi on the same day – April 1, 1944. They stood victorious again, but suffered 200 casualties in the battle for Luzon.

The rice fields of Luzon, where the 158th Bushmasters would make a push toward Manila.

(5239)   Bontoc Cervantes Road, Cabunagan Section Km. 418 Bontoc Mt. Province 2-20-34 (B. PW.)

Steve Zozaya, a member of Post 41, was one of those who despite injuries survived the battle. Not fond of reliving war stories, Zozaya did share the experience briefly in a 2004 interview.

"We were in the front line where we'd been battling. There were other troops that got ahead of us. Anyway, there was a wounded man. Two of them in fact, in front of us. And we could hear him. 'Help! Help!' And, so I just jumped up and I ran. And I got to maybe about 30 yards. I got up and the man was there. The other man was already gone.

"So I crawled. I got him to get up on my back. I got up and I was running back with him when the mortars hit. And they just knocked me down, hit my legs."

Zozaya would survive his experience, receiving the Bronze Star and a Purple Heart for his efforts. He would return home to become one of Phoenix's most prominent Latinos.[19]

The original 1940s patch for the Bushmasters 158th Infantry Regiment.

The 158th continued its island-hopping advance toward the Philippines, eating away at Japanese territory with unlauded efficiency. Sorsogon. Camalig. Mt. Isarog. Yokohama. MacArthur checked off names on the map as they advanced. One of their greatest challenges would be Noemfoor in July 1944.

With three airbases and a well-used staging area for Japanese troop deployment, the island of Noemfoor was a strategic point that needed to be eliminated for Allied success. On July 2, MacArthur chose the 158th to spearhead what he called Operation Cyclone. Joined by the British Royal Air Force and five other U.S. fighter and bombardment groups, Operation Cyclone totaled more than 8,000 men.

The morning of July 2 the men of the 158th were flown to the beaches of Noemfoor near Kamiri airfield by Task Force 77.

Though the three airfields were captured within five days, the rogue Japanese mounted a guerilla campaign that dragged through Aug. 31, 1944.

By August of the following year, the 158th Regimental Combat Team was being called on to spearhead one last hard attack – an invasion into Japan's own territories. Back home, families in the barrio read the newspapers nervously as their men pushed on.

On the home front

In 1943, Los Angeles was a hotbed of news around the nation as young Mexican Americans and U.S. sailors clashed. Known as the Zoot Suit Riots, the incident was the explosion of emotions that had grown from a build-up of violence and racial tensions in the Chavez Ravine community.

Back in Phoenix, people waited and worried. They had experienced similar tension. A riot among soldiers in Phoenix on Feb. 27, 1942, led to the death of several Black soldiers and raised the community's wariness around minorities. Hispanic families did their best to avoid confrontations.

As 1943 came to a close and Christmas approached, tragic news continued to roll in. The Lara household was heartbroken when word came of its son's death. Ray Lara had died in action in Africa. Two days before, his young wife had given birth to a son.[20]

To help their soldiers and perhaps keep themselves distracted from the heartbreak, the South Phoenix barrios showed support for the troops in numerous ways.

In February 1944, Immaculate Heart of Mary Catholic Church opened its doors for the annual nine-day pre-Lenten novena prayer services. The church's chronicle recorded the event asking for the safety of the soldiers from their parish. Each night, the church was packed with parishioners, depositing their prayer items. Soon, hundreds of soldiers' photographs surrounded the church's holy crucifix. Three hundred and fifty candles were lit, day and night.

On the final night, more than 900 parishioners came to receive communion.[21]

The following year, in March 1945, the Battle of the Bulge was a tragedy recent in their memories. The Russians were unveiling the atrocities at Auschwitz. And the war continued to come home in heartbreaking moments such as the POW letter from Pete Dimas and Silvestre Herrera's valiant but tragic loss. But these weren't the ultimate sacrifice.

The death toll of Arizona soldiers early that year was 22. Pfc. Hilario Padilla and Sgt. Hilario M. Gutierrez of Phoenix were listed among the dead.

Immaculate Heart again received the community en masse for novena. Another 700 photographs were placed in the church and there were nearly 200 more candles than the year before.[22]

But the barrio did not just pray for its sons and daughters in the war. Families, organizations, entire barrios were involved in the war effort from the beginning. As early as Jan. 30, 1942, Los Leñadores del Mundo (Woodsmen of the World) held a "Diamond Jubilee" dance and festival to honor President Roosevelt and to show Mexican support for the war effort.[23]

In July, there was a nationwide crisis of the oil supply as the new plastics industry struggled to keep up with the needed production of war materials. The Standard Oil Company challenged several communities to gather as much plastic as they could in a competition. In Arizona, the kids of the Marcos De Niza housing project scoured their streets for anything made of the precious material. They managed to gather 2,200 pounds – more than any other youth group in Phoenix.[24]

As the winter of 1942 approached, Phoenix began to feel another shortage. Its huge cotton industry was again at risk, and it was needed for war production of parachutes, blimps and gliders. With some local Mexican American organizations helping – such as La Alianza Hispano Americana and Los Leñadores – the Victory Labor Volunteer Group organized a three-week harvest. As many as 5,000 Mexican American workers stepped in to pick 35,000 pounds of cotton before the crop was lost. White and brown skin worked side by side in the fields to finish the job with patriotism flush in their faces.[25]

Realizing the passion and potential of the Hispanic community, a February 1943 meeting was held by leaders of Spanish-speaking churches in Phoenix. They decided to take active parts in pushing the Hispanic community to continue its involvement in such local war efforts. Local Spanish-language newspapers *El*

Mensajero and *El Sol* helped get the word out.[26]

The following year those efforts paid off. An event was organized with mariachis, folk dancers, food and celebration. At its core, this "Noche Mexicana" was a bond drive. Kicking off this effort, the Immaculate Heart of Mary Church's pastor stepped forward as the first to purchase a bond for $500. *El Sol* bought the second bond. Several other Mexican American businesses followed, at $500 each.

When the night was over, $90,000 in bond money had been raised. The drive continued on to raise more than $200,000.[27]

Children continued to roam the streets, collecting rubber, cigarettes and money for war bonds. Stories of the community participation continued to be trumpeted in *El Mensajero* and lauded in *El Sol*. Newspaper articles told the story of the war, and kept readers abreast as to what their sons and daughters were facing. One publication printed a full page detailing the soldiers

And so, the community passed the time. People stayed busy, honoring their loved ones in the war. Waiting for them to come home. Through the early months of 1945, Germany slowly came under Allied control. In the second half of 1945, the U.S. government would add an unprecedented page to the history books in its effort to force Japan into submission.

A blinding flash
and a violent blast

On the last day of April, 1945, Hitler sat in a bunker with his new bride, Eva Braun, at his side. The Russians were two blocks away. His Italian counterpart Benito Mussolini had been hanged. Across the countryside, his military forces were surrendering.

In the enormity of his genocidal reign, it is ironic that Hitler personally killed just one person during World War II – himself. Within days, his closest companions had fled, committed suicide or were captured. The Nazi regime had crumbled.

In January, after having reached the beaches of Luzon, commanders began exploring the possibilities of pushing an attack into Japan's main islands. In May 1945, formal planning began on what would be called Operation Downfall. The Bushmasters 158th was slated as the hard edge of this campaign, detailing its invasion of islands just south of Kyushu on Oct. 27.[28]

This would never happen. A worried U.S. government feared the expansion of Communist Russia, as it pushed toward Japan from the north. Admiral William Leahy gave a frightening number of possible casualties he expected in the attack. He predicted 250,000 Americans would be killed or injured just on the island of Kyushu. Another general suggested the entire operation could cost one million lives.

The time had come to pull a deadly card the U.S. had been holding for four years.

When Ralph Chavarria of Phoenix joined the fight two and a half years before, he could not have known he'd be on hand for one of modern history's most important moments. Drafted at age 27, he would serve as a firefighter on Tinian in the Northern Mariana Islands in Micronesia and see no combat, though he was on deck for trips to sea when a pilot had crashed into the ocean.

Long before the sun rose on Aug. 9, 1945, he and his crew stood at the end of a runway on Tinian Island, just as they had three days before. "At five-minute intervals, three planes would take off. All we thought was 'suppose the plane would not take off (and) crash here, what would happen to this island?'" he recalled 60 years later.[29]

Chavarria's fears were well founded. A bomb nicknamed Fat Boy was stowed on the B-29 that sped down the runway and up into the night sky. Three days before, the world had been stunned by the first atomic bomb detonation in Hiroshima. For hours just one message was transmitted from somewhere outside of Hiroshima, describing Fat Boy's deadly brother, Little Man, "violent, large special-type bomb, giving the appearance of magnesium." It had exploded with a "blinding flash and a violent blast."

At 11:02 a.m. three days later, Fat Boy was detonated over Nagasaki and 75,000 Japanese died. Six days later, Japan surrendered.

By war's end, 1,875 Arizona soldiers had died in World War II. More than 600 were from Maricopa County. Scan a list of the fallen, and a large number have recognizably Hispanic surnames. (At least 150 in Maricopa County).[30]

Nobody truly knows how many Hispanic Americans and Mexicans served during World War II. The U.S. War Dept. kept no known record of Hispanics who served in the armed forces – except Puerto Ricans (53,000 served between 1940-46). But some scholars have come to the conclusion that between 375,000 and 500,000 Latinos and Latino Americans joined from across the U.S. When considering they were only 3 percent of the American population at the time, this is a notable number[31] – 2.5 million Mexican Americans lived in the United States in 1940.

Boeing B-29 Superfortress "Enola Gay" landing on Tinian island after the atomic bombing mission on Hiroshima, Japan. (U.S. Air Force photo)

PHOTO COURTESY U.S. AIR FORCE ARCHIVES

The men come home

"**W**e got to the Statue of Liberty. Then we landed and they had bands playing and everything else. We kissed the ground. We didn't know what to do. And then we went to Camp Hamilton. And they had a big cake on the table and they had good stuff there. With a sign that said, 'Welcome home, heroes!' in the middle of the table."[32]

That is how Sgt. Pete Dimas remembered his homecoming from World War II. After four months in a prison camp, he'd been rescued in April 1945.

Many felt as American as ever. They glowed in the heroes' welcome.

Silvestre Herrera, Arizona's first WWII Medal of Valor honoree, was lavished with the most attention when he came home that August. Gov. Sydney P. Osborn announced August 14, 1945, to be "Herrera Day." and had businesses along Central Avenue remove signs saying "No Mexican Trade Wanted." A parade was organized in Herrera's honor. Phoenicians started a donation drive and raised almost $14,000 to provide him and his family a new home.[33]

But other heroes, such as Mike Gomez, found only a quiet train platform when they returned home. No crowd – just anxious families waiting at the station to greet their arrival.

"You had to prepare yourself when returning: There was no one to receive you," Gomez said, referring to his arrival by train in Phoenix. "Only the family. Luckily, we Latinos have more unity." His family hadn't seen him in some time. His wife paced nervously when she was unable to recognize which soldier was her husband.[34]

"I had to point to myself and say 'It's me, it's me!'" Gomez recalls with a laugh.

Once Silvestre Herrera's ticker-tape parade was over and the marching bands went home, Latino soldiers looked around to find nothing had truly changed for them. Their barrios still stood in dust and basic survival mode; still ignored by the city proper.

When the war ended, many people lost their jobs and returned to working the crop fields. But their challenges were far more than employment, or being forced to sit in the back balcony at a movie theater.

The day these men returned from World War II, Phoenix did not open its doors wide to them as they might have expected. They were still locked out of housing opportunities. Segregation had its grip on the Latino population, similar to other minorities. Many of the communities occupied by Latinos, African Americans and Asians were on the southern fringes of Phoenix. A sense of patriotic inclusion made some forget they were not welcome. They were swiftly reminded.

Ralph Chavarria came home to his wife, Consuelo, and his son, Ernie, in 1946. His brother joined him at a central Phoenix bar to enjoy a couple 25 cent beers. But they had to pay $2 for the cold brew.

"So then, we ordered more," Ralph explained in an interview with a local newspaper "And here comes a big, old, fat man. He came back without beer and said, 'Can't you read between the lines?' The prejudice was still there."[35]

But sometimes Latinos were reminded of the scorn much more painfully. Old Vincent Canales and his wife, who owned the Ramona Drug Store, joined their son, Armando, and the rest of the family for a few drinks at the Pekoe Club on south Central Avenue. They were out to celebrate their son's return from the war. He had suffered three long years in Japanese prison camps after being captured on the island of Corregidor.

With such joy on their minds, they couldn't have expected the night would turn bitter. But several in the crowd were angered that these Mexican Americans had ventured into their bar for a drink. Soon an altercation became a fight and, in the confines of the nightclub, the Canales were faced with a hateful mob. The crowd surged toward them.

Most escaped with minor cuts and bruises. But after having survived tragedies as a prisoner of war, Armando was sent to the hospital with severe injuries suffered in his own country. Two men were arrested, but the instigators of the mob seemed to have slipped into the night undetected.[36]

Housing segregation in Phoenix had been practiced informally for many years, creating areas such as South Phoenix. But the National Housing Act of 1934 allowed the Home Owners' Loan Corporation to create maps that showed what they percieved as high-risk areas for banks lending money. Outlined in red, these danger zones consistently included minority neighborhoods. Banks would then base their lending decisions on these maps, denying mortgage loans to people living within the red-lined areas.

With no money coming for improvements to homes, or for the building of new homes, these poorer neighborhoods began to decline further.

In 1944, the G.I. Bill was created, giving numerous opportunities to soldiers returning from WWII – including guaranteed mortgage loans, job training, and money to cover times of unemployment.

Minority veterans would apply for the benefits in hopes of buying a new home, often in the clean, modern suburbs that were growing around Phoenix. But realtors would avoid selling to minorities, fearing they might lose business from the Anglo community, and that neighborhoods with minorities would lose value.

In 1968, the Fair Housing Act would help eliminate discriminatory practices. The Community Reinvestment Act of 1977 would help further, by effectively eliminating discriminatory red-lining practices.

Others, though spared physical harm, found they were refused one of life's most basic needs: a home.

After battling through the jungles of the Philippines and across the islands of a volatile Japanese empire, the Bushmasters had returned to Arizona as the state's pride and joy. And hoping to rediscover normal life. One member of the 158th, David Perez, decided to use his G.I. Bill to finance a home for his family.

He stepped into an office of the Valley National Bank and waited for the loan officer to speak with him. When Perez explained his desire to buy a home and held out his military certificate, the man was supportive. "Get a good quote, prints. Get bids on the house and then come back."

Perez was thrilled. He tracked down an architect and worked on a bid to build their new home. When he got a low bid of $4,500, he felt the cards had fallen in his favor, "Oh! Got it made!" He returned to the bank and dropped off his paperwork with the loan officer.

But when the loan officer called him, Perez fell victim to the city's social taboos. "Sorry, Mr. Perez, but we don't finance anything south of the tracks – south of Washington."

David Perez gave a wry smile in one interview shortly before his passing in 2004, and explained it succinctly. "At that time, we couldn't buy north of the downtown area anyhow. And they wouldn't finance south. So it was like a fish without a bowl. What you gonna do? You got the certificate. But no one to take it."[37]

These circumstances inspired the founding of Post 41.

Organizing toward a goal

In 1945, the American Legion Luke-Greenway Post 1 was the largest in Arizona and the only post in Phoenix. Founded in 1919 at the same time as the national organization, the post sat north of Van Buren Street on 7th Avenue, near Grand Avenue. Some Latinos joined the post after returning from World War II, but they were never truly welcomed. They were tolerated, but sensing the risk of outright racism, the Latino veterans decided to find their own way. And they had a goal.

War changes people. It revises their perspective of the world. Latino veterans returned to Phoenix wanting to achieve what they deserved: equal opportunity for their families and inclusion in all aspects of the greater community. They felt they were partners in the Great American Democratic experiment, now more than ever. To achieve these ends, they used the best tool learned on the battlefields of World War II. They organized.

Ray Martinez had come home in October 1945 after his tour of duty as a radio operator on the USS Makassar Strait, an escort carrier operating in the Pacific on numerous missions from Okinawa to the Philippines.

Ray had begun rekindling some of his old friendships with other veterans who had also returned to the barrio. One was Frank "Pipa" Fuentes, a rebellious youth who had become Arizona's welterweight boxing champion for a time, then quit his job as a railroad signal operator in 1943 to fight in the war.

PHOTO COURTESY OF THE CHICANO COLLECTION, DEPARTMENT OF ARCHIVES AND SPECIAL COLLECTIONS, ARIZONA STATE UNIVERSITY

Ray Martinez, standing third from right, was a recreation director with the Madison Street Settlement before entering the war. Here poses with his baseball team.

Fuentes had a proposal.

After the cold reception from American Legion Post 1, Frank Fuentes decided to organize an American Legion post where Latinos would feel welcome. He was gathering veterans to help; Pete Martinez, Pete G. Dimas, Carlos Ontiveros, Phil Fierros, Alex Delgado, Ruben M. Parra and others had already joined the effort. They invited Martinez to join. Their ideas intrigued him.

When Frank spoke with Ray, the group had already begun the early steps to convince the American Legion to provide them with a charter for their own post. Frank Fuentes attempted to obtain a new charter from the Arizona American Legion office. Discussions began over whether or not there should be a separate post for Mexican Americans, and the charter application was stalled in the state legion's executive committee.

"They were a little suspicious," Ray Martinez recalled in a 1980 interview. "I guess they thought we were going to open up a beer club and have fights and gambling."[38]

Solidarity and persistence would help them achieve their goals. The new post was eventually approved and the new American Legion Thunderbird Post 41 received its charter by November 1945, creating Arizona's first Hispanic post and the second post in Phoenix at the time.

Ray Martinez would later remind interviewers on many occasions that the goal had always been much more than simply founding a place for camaraderie. "When we got out of the service, some of us knew, we had a mission, because we were not going to go back to the discrimination we had suffered before. We knew that was the time, right after the war, everybody had a good feeling, everybody loved the service men and (we) thought, well this is the time to make the move."[39]

Nor were they alone in their ideas. At the dawn of the baby boom generation, human rights had become a focus for many. In 1946, the Congress of American Women organized to fight for women's rights in the U.S. The Civil Rights Congress was also formed to help Blacks living in Detroit. Like magnets to their cause, activists began to unite.

The Hispanic community was no exception. In Texas, the American G.I. Forum was formed in 1948 by Hispanic Americans. In southern California, unity leagues fought injustices against impoverished minorities.

Segregation was an issue being met head-on across the nation as minorities became empowered and educated. But Post 41 was special in that these were barrio kids who'd come home. Many had no college degrees; most had no high school diplomas. They were factory workers and farm workers. And none of them truly had any idea how to run an American Legion post.

They had no building yet. Frank Fuentes offered to shut down his family's restaurant one night a week for their meetings. And so on Tuesdays the small group of 16 members converged on 2nd Street and Jefferson to sit in the dining room of La Poblanita restaurant. Carlos Ontiveros was briefly commander. Then after receiving the charter, Ray Martinez was voted in, officially becoming the first Hispanic commander of an Arizona American Legion post. Frank Fuentes served as chaplain, a post he held consistently until becoming commander in 1955.

In the first meeting, they discussed the poverty in their neighborhoods and the discrimination their families were enduring. Their thoughts were jotted down on a napkin. They may not have learned yet how to run an American Legion post, but it was clear what their agenda would be. Ray explaines, "We talked about how to organize because there was a lot of discrimination against Mexicans and we thought it was time to start fighting back... Discrimination (was) the number one issue. We wanted a piece of the pie, too."[40]

And they would not be alone in their fight. As the napkin filled with ideas, one of Frank Fuentes' old grade school buddies, a young man named Barry, looked on. As he'd grown, the youth was obsessed with learning to fly airplanes and eventually became the politically active general manager of a local department store. And here he was, at Post 41. In time he would be known to the world as Sen. Barry Goldwater. The same year the post received its charter, Goldwater had returned as a brigadier general in the U.S. Air Force and helped to organize the 158th into the new Arizona National Guard. He had been courting politics, but found that, despite growing up in his mother's Episcopalian faith, his Jewish heritage was given the same cold shoulder as other minorities. Goldwater saw in the Latino cause something that could help his own.

Despite the group's lack of experience as legionnaires, they had some experience in social issues. Before joining the fight in World War II, Ray Martinez had already been involved in community activities as a recreation director at the Madison Street Settlement on 9th Street and Madison.[41]

To raise money for baseball and other events at Madison Park, Ray would gather a handful of his boxing students and take them to the Biltmore shopping mall. They would set up a boxing ring and put on a show. People tossed money into the ring, which the young boxers scooped up to help aid their cause.[42]

A decade later, as Post 41 was fast becoming an institution in the community, one might argue that the roots of its success could be found in the social networking of pre-war gatherings such as those at Madison Street Settlement. Ray drew on his experience to create programs for the community.

By 1947, the post was supporting one of Ray and Frank's joys – a local boxing team they coached.[43] Heavyweight boxer Manuel Larios from Phoenix College would win the 1948 Arizona Golden Gloves tournament by knocking his opponent down three times – in the second round. That year, their boxing team walked away with four championships and another reaching the finals.[44] In January 1948, they headed to Los Angeles to compete in the regional competition.

But as 1947 ended, the men of Post 41 had done much more than teach young boxers. They had partnered with a sorority and the local Campfire Girls office to send six girls from Grant Park community to a summer camp in Prescott for 10 days. Post 41 was also providing transportation for softball teams from both Grant and Harmon parks and organized blood

Ray Martinez and the boxing team he coached with Pipa Fuentes on their way to Los Angeles to compete in the Division Golden Gloves Boxing tournament.

drives. They held dances several times a year. During the fall they began holding an annual barbecue at Grant Park. It brought everyone in the community together.[45]

The battlefields of Asia and Europe were now a memory, and the members of Post 41 would begin earning respect through the civilian battles they fought. Their first challenge was a swimming pool in Tempe.

Unshared waters

In 1923, Tempe finished construction of its first recreation facilities: Tempe Beach Park. Built near a popular swimming area used since 1916, it was the city's attempt to avoid drowning and the threat of disease that came with swimming in the river or nearby canals. The result was an Olympic-size creation, hosting swim meets that brought young athletes from across the Southwest to compete.[46]

It also brought a boy named Ray Martinez, living in Tempe. The children in the Tempe barrios had heard there was a new pool being built. When construction had completed and the pool was ready for use, all the children came to see their new treasure. But when Ray walked up to the gate, there was a sign: "No dogs or Mexicans allowed." The pool was off-limits – a policy enforced by the Tempe Chamber of Commerce and sanctioned by the City of Tempe.[47]

Remarkably few complaints were made against the policy for almost 20 years. Most members of the Hispanic community found satisfaction swimming in the open canal on Price Road or trekking to the rapids at Blue Point on the Salt River, when it flowed.[48] The complaints that were voiced often went unanswered and unsolved. One example is when a St. Mary's girls club traveled to Tempe Beach in hopes of having a picnic. Several chaperones traveled with them, including Lillie Perez's mother.

When the manager refused entry to Lillie and her mother, based on the segregation policy, the priests and chaperones tried to gain entrance, explaining that Lillie was a good kid who had never been rejected entry from anywhere before. Little girls are harmless. As justification, some of the ladies gestured past the arched cobblestone entry at two other Mexican children who had been allowed to swim – Adeline and Pauline Loza.[49]

After the manager spun around to spot the two kids that had gone in undetected, they were thrown out as well.

Even though Rev. M. Ignatius of St. Mary's Church sent a disapproving letter that detailed the event, the problem would not be solved until the 1940s.

Tempe Beach pool, in the 1950s.

PHOTO COURTESY OF TEMPE HISTORICAL MUSEUM

In 1942, the Tempe Chamber of Commerce turned over control and management of Tempe Beach to a new Tempe Beach Committee.[50] In early June, another incident spurred an attempt for even harder pool desegregation. The League of United Latin American Citizens (LULAC), Council 110, stepped forward to take up this cause.

Two Mexican American women had gone to the pool on a date with Mexican Air Force cadets training at Williams Air Force Base. The cadets were part of a group from several South and Central American countries that had been included in the military effort, possibly to reinforce President Roosevelt's "Good Neighbor Policy" and show Latin American support for the U.S. during the war.[51]

Before World War II, the "Good Neighbor Policy" was Roosevelt's attempt at repairing severely damaged relationships with Latin American countries and to prevent the world's unstable politics and violence from reaching U.S. soil. Unfortunately, a grand U.S. policy does not always spread into small communities with contradictory views.

PHOTO COURTESY OF TEMPE HISTORICAL MUSEUM

Mayor William W. Cole of Tempe, (1937 – 1948) refused to step in to help desegregate the Tempe Beach Pool.

Word of the latest Tempe Pool incident reached Maria A. Garcia, head of LULAC Council 110's Phoenix Discrimination Committee. She contacted Placida Garcia Smith at Friendly House. Together they notified the members of their LULAC council. The Phoenix Discrimination Committee was given the go-ahead to investigate the incident further and share what it found. It was perfect timing. There was an opportunity later that month to report the findings at the 1942 LULAC convention in Albuquerque, N.M. But they had to act quickly.

Garcia and her committee secured a meeting with Tempe Mayor W.W. Cole. As the meeting began, Garcia told Cole that their discussion would be brought up at the upcoming national LULAC convention. Then she voiced the committee's displeasure with the treatment of the young Mexican American women and the Mexican cadets, reminding the mayor of President Roosevelt's "Good Neighbor Policy."

But the mayor was unfazed. He took his stance bluntly: The city had no control over the park's policies because Tempe had simple-leased the land to the Tempe Chamber of Commerce which was beyond the city's "jurisdiction" and made its own rules and regulations. He could not help her.

Finding their grievances blocked at the mayor's office, the committee next approached Max Connolly, president of the Tempe Chamber of Commerce. Again they were stopped short. Connolly flatly refused to make any changes without the approval of the chamber board and the Tempe Beach Committee.[52]

Garcia was true to her word. At the national LULAC conference in Albuquerque, she related the ineffective meeting. New Mexico Sen. Dennis Chavez was on hand to hear Council 110's concerns about the Tempe Beach incident. Sen. Chavez had been integral to the creation of the "Good Neighbor Policy" and also was a cousin to Placida Garcia-Smith of the Friendly House.

On June 14 in Albuquerque, Chavez spoke at a LULAC dedication ceremony of the Barelas Community Center. There he called on LULAC members to bring to light any occurrence of discrimination in their local communities. He explained that they had the "backing of the entire nation in its will to promote friendly relations in Latin America."[53]

Chavez made no direct mention of the pool incident, but the local Council 110 felt inspired nonetheless. The council sought out the two women who had been turned down at Tempe Beach and obtained legal affidavits describing what had occurred.

Council 110 had begun to increase community pressure. But the Tempe Beach Committee continued to slip out of their hands, denying the changes LULAC desired.

In 1943, a federal court ruled Tempe Beach's segregation was unconstitutional. But the Tempe Beach Committee continued to stand by its segregation and defiance of the ruling.

It believed the federal ruling was irrelevant to swimming pool regulations because it was a citizen's committee, and no laws had been broken. Indeed, no city laws had even been written to desegregate Tempe Beach. The pool area was still off-limits to Hispanics.[54]

As more pressure was applied by LULAC, the committee deflected its efforts. Rather than integrate the pool, the Tempe Beach Committee announced that it had reserved $500 "for the purpose of constructing a second swimming pool for the exclusive use of the citizens of Mexican extraction." They then asked the Tempe City Council to donate land for this new pool.

Not only was the desegregation issue being dodged, the idea was never feasible. It came at a time when the U.S. was asking for anything communities could offer help in the war effort. The city of Tempe certainly wasn't going to authorize needed materials to build a second pool.

A priest at Tempe Catholic Church, Rev. Bernard Gordon, attempted to help. In late November 1944, he held a fundraising drive to collect the money needed to build another pool in Tempe. But he was unsuccessful and the alternate pool was never built.[55]

The LULAC council found its attempts stalled at every turn. The decades-old policy refused to die. They needed help.

Three men approached Post 41 soon after it had received its charter; Danny Rodriguez, Raymond Terminal and Genaro Martinez. It was known throughout the Latino community that Post 41 had formed in hopes of making a difference. The Post's new commander, Ray Martinez, listened as they explained how LULAC's attempts at desegregation had been derailed.

A long discussion followed among the members of Post 41. What could or would they do? Ray Martinez was asked to be chairman of the effort. Then a plan of action was agreed upon. Post 41's involvement would stay behind the scenes. Being outsiders from Phoenix could damage the cause.

The first step would be to meet with each member individually, taking away the Tempe Beach Committee's safety in numbers and group mentality. This would make it easier for the post and the Tempe veterans to explain why the "No Mexicans" policy was wrong and sway their vote at an upcoming meeting to decide if the rules would be changed.

Dwight "Red" Harkins in the 1930s. He founded Harkins Theatre, and often supported Post 41 in its efforts.

PHOTO COURTESY OF TEMPE HISTORICAL MUSEUM

Meanwhile, friendships were built with outspoken and important businessmen in Tempe to gain backing for their cause. Connections were beginning to grow in the community, providing much of the influence Post 41 would hold in the coming years.

The first to step forward in support was Dwight "Red" Harkins, who had begun his movie theater business 13 years before and eventually developed a solid connection to Phoenix Latino communities when he married the former Alice Peralta. Then Lawrence and Mittie Carr, two brothers that owned Carr Mortuary, joined Harkins. The Curry twins followed. Michael and Edward Jr. ran the Tempe hardware store their father had started in 1889 on south Mill in downtown Tempe. These were the respected names of Tempe life, and they were backing the desegregation cause.

As these relationships formed, they were able to whittle their opponents down to two chamber members who could never be convinced to allow integration of the pool. Harrold Nevitt, a service station owner and Reginald J.H. Stroud.

Ray Martinez was told of a chamber meeting that became heated when Stroud and Harkins sparred:

"Dr. Stroud said: 'If you allow these Mexicans in there, they're gonna tear the damn place up! We won't be able to keep up with the damage!' And Dwight "Red" Harkins said: 'Well, how much damage do you think they'll make?' And Dr. Stroud said, 'At least $10,000 worth!' So, I heard that Dwight "Red" Harkins wrote him out a check for the $10,000 and said: 'Look. Here's a check. I'm going to give it to you. If they tear up the place, you can go ahead and cash my check and pay for the damages. But only for damages for the place.' They say that after Dr. Stroud died and they were processing his paper work, they found that $10,000 check. It was still there."[56]

Eventually a date was set to vote on the issue: May 21, 1946.

In the days leading up to the vote, Arizona State College joined the fight. Barbara Crumpler, president of the local Beta Phi chapter of Kappa Delta Pi, wrote a letter to the Tempe Beach Committee urging integration at their pool.

"In the interests of true democracy, we urge that admission to the Tempe Beach swimming pool be on the basis of cleanliness rather than on racial differences. Representing as you do the citizens of Tempe, we feel that you cannot help recognizing the injustice of the present un-American practice of refusing to admit clean and decent citizens of Mexican heritage."[70]

With a successful first step, the next was to join the Tempe Chamber of Commerce and begin several debates over segregation. Ramón Padilla and Genaro Martinez, two of the men who had approached Post 41 for their help, announced their desire to join the chamber of commerce in May; the same month that the chamber was to vote on desegregation of the pool.

Ramon and Genaro lobbied members to accept them into the chamber's folds. As a backup plan if their membership was voted against, "Red" Harkins set aside $2,500 for Ray Martinez of Post 41 to use in hiring a lawyer to file a desegregation lawsuit against the chamber.[59]

The money was never needed.

On May 21, 1946, Genaro Martinez, Danny Rodriguez and Ramon Padilla were admitted as members of the Tempe Chamber of Commerce. In the same meeting, the "No Mexicans Allowed" policy was stopped by a vote of 15-14.[61]

The Tempe and Phoenix veterans thought their fight was over. But they faced one more hurdle.

The policy had been changed, but the chamber made a move to put new stipulations in place. The pool was to be open on a limited basis, and some members spoke of restricting use of the pool to residents of Tempe only. The Tempe Beach Committee was still in charge and deciding who "qualified" for admission to the swimming pool. This was still unacceptable, and another vote was planned, days later.[62]

The dean of Arizona State College (ASU), J.O. Grimes, would type up his concerns and advised subversively that the restrictions were inappropriate by suggesting that restrictions were a good idea. He then suggested non-racial restrictions: "Cleanliness of skin rather than color of skin should be the accepted basic principle for entrance to any pool. Cleanliness of conduct should be the second criteria."

On the day of the new vote, numerous absentees made the hopes of full equality seem distant. None from the community appeared. Danny Rodriguez stood alone before the committee asking them to vote in favor.

In a narrow victory, the pool was opened to all races. The Tempe veterans and American Legion Post 41 had succeeded.[63] Finally, three years after the federal court had outlawed segregation at the pool, it was opened to all. Almost a quarter century of exclusion had ended.

The achievement did come with a cost. Danny Rodriguez found himself blackballed after the effort. He received threats and couldn't find a job.[64]

He soon found it necessary to move. In a 1993 interview by David Solliday, Tempe resident Ray Chavarria shed some light on one reason he might have left: the lack of support when he needed it most. The entire Hispanic community was behind him 100 percent, but Danny's view of the community changed after he'd stood before the court alone.

"He went that morning. How do you think that Danny must have felt, to have the people supporting, encourage him and everything, and he gets all the information he can together, compiles it to make his presentation, and he goes to the courtroom, and he starts looking, and none of his people from the barrios were there. And then the judge calls him to make his presentation. He made such a wonderful presentation that he won! (Was he suing the city?) Yes, I think he was. I can't recall what it was, but he was left alone.

"He must have felt very lonely. When he walked out of (the chamber meeting), he must have really walked out with a lot of bitterness, because Danny moved away from Tempe. And some of us, I don't know who may know where he's at. But he was one of the heroes, another individual, really heroes, when prejudice and discrimination was practiced in Tempe."[65]

Soon after the changes took place, his 7-year-old niece, Becky, caught him gazing into the desegregated pool as she swam. Worried, she asked what he was doing. Danny looked up at her: "I'm looking at a change of time. And it is good."

A home for every veteran

When soldiers came home from World War II, the legendary housing boom had not quite begun in Phoenix. The entire Valley was still recovering from a sudden shift of focus during the war. The area had become a main production center for equipment needed in the war effort. Now that the war was over, the local economy had to swerve in a new direction yet again. One resource that continued to be scarce was housing for the workers. Many communities had to build temporary housing to provide for the workers.

These problems had begun to grow severe during the Depression years. Now that the war had ended, soldiers across the nation were coming home and finding themselves forced to live in tents, street cars or worse.

In Phoenix, Ray Martinez, the commander of Post 41, saw the barrios suffering as well. "During the war, there was a shortage of housing. And after the war, veterans came home and they had to double up with others. I mean, there's 10 or 12 living to a house, and we were very much concerned about it, and so were the officials."[66]

Everyone was suffering. Not just Hispanics. In early 1946, the Veterans' Emergency Housing Program was formed to battle the problem. Congress made funds available to municipalities so that veteran housing could be built. When they were told they could receive 150 pre-fab homes to use for emergency housing in Phoenix, city officials voted to provide them at three different sites.

One hundred homes for Anglo veterans would be built near downtown.

Twenty five homes for African American veterans near the Mathew T. Henson Housing Project in South Phoenix.

Then they announced where the Hispanic veterans military housing would be placed. The next challenge was about to begin for Thunderbird Post 41.

Like crossing a new beachhead, Ray Martinez dove forward, challenging the status quo. There would be no acting behind the scenes, as with the Tempe Beach issue.

The Anglo homes were to be placed at an abandoned Civilian Conservation Corps camp on 10 acres, near 809 N. 19th Street in the Garfield housing community. The Mexican American units were tentatively planned for the site of an old city dump at 5th Street and Henshaw Road (present-day Buckeye Road).[67]

On March 23, 1946, Ray Martinez voiced his concerns to City Manager Roy Heyne. Promises were made "to cover the dump; landscape it, and make it look pretty."[34] But this was unacceptable to the Mexican American veterans. It was unsanitary, with open-air toilets and contamination. Nor was it even large enough to provide space for yards. Ray suggested putting the houses at Harmon Park near the Marcos de Niza project or that they be integrated into the 10 acres of land where the Anglos were to be located.[69]

The city agreed to cooperate with Post 41, and Ray spoke before the municipal parks board to ask that Harmon Park be made available as a site for the project.

Phoenix Mayor Ray Busey (1946-1948) proved helpful to the minority cause. Before he left office he created the Charter Government Committee.

PHOTO COURTESY OF ARIZONA HISTORICAL SOCIETY

City officials instead elected to combine the Mexican American homes with the 16th and Roosevelt street project. The city engineer cited excessive costs of installing utilities at the proposed Mexican American location as the reason their idea was abandoned.[70]

Anglo property owners in the Garfield neighborhood quickly became uncomfortable with the idea of Mexican Americans moving in. They banded together with Anglo veterans to form the Garfield Property Owners Protective Association. Eddie H. Poole, a fellow veteran who had fought at Iwo Jima, was to be the organization's leader against integration.

Eddie Poole stood before the Phoenix City Council and denounced the idea as a travesty in his eyes. Ray Martinez was there to witness his words. "My God it was the most awful thing you would want to hear," he said. "'Those damn Mexicans, you put them in there, they're gonna be raping, they're gonna be robbing and you know, we're going to have all kinds of problems. And we just don't want them because we need to protect our families.' It was so terrible that the members of the city council were just absolutely devastated, you could see that they were completely uncomfortable. When you start using language that rough, well then that's what can cause riots."[71]

When Ray's time came, he stood and explained the absurdity of such an argument. He reminded them that they had all fought together. Why couldn't they live together?

Suddenly, another man stood up. Kenny Rosenbaum. He was a Jewish lawyer and a member of B'nai B'rith. "My goodness, here we are. We've just been through a war that was mainly motivated by hate, and here we have somebody still spewing hate as bad as Hitler did over there."[72]

Then labor leader John Dutch rose up and Communist party leader Morris Graham. The two defended Ray as an upright citizen and supported integrated housing projects.

The city council took a brief recess to think things over. Whereas Ray and his supporters had spoken reasonably, they were still stung by the harsh words of Eddie Poole. Fifteen minutes later the council members returned to make their announcement. "The city council has decided to take this entire matter into consideration. And we'll decide at a later date." Ray Martinez would not find the answer he sought that day.

But it was an election year, Ray remembers. "The council was voted out. Ray Busey was elected mayor and they immediately said, 'Integrate it. It goes together.'"

Going down hard

The decision was made to allow 24 of the Garfield site's federal housing units to go to Mexican American veterans. Prefabricated housing that had been in use during the war was loaded on trains and shipped from the state of Washington and from Bisbee to be used in Phoenix for the project.

No time was wasted. On July 2 Eddie Poole and members of the community argued before the city commissioners and the new mayor of Phoenix, explaining that the integration of Mexican Americans into their area would lower property values and invite crime into their community.

Phoenix Mayor Ray Busey had just taken office in June 1946. He was an unexpected windfall at the time for Ray Martinez and the members of Post 41. He knew Spanish. He spoke on behalf of Black pastors and the disabled. He had already been involved in numerous civil betterment groups and was in constant communication with Emmett McLoughlin, the most powerful social activist in Phoenix at the time.[73]

And in the face of Poole's demands, Mayor Busey stood his ground. The project was to continue. He explained that their concerns were minor because the housing was only temporary. The federal government contract stated that the temporary housing would be removed within two years of the end of the housing crisis.

Soon the meeting became a shouting match. John Dutch and Morris Graham spoke out in support of integration. Others would not have it.

Even a local church leader joined the fray against the Hispanic veterans. The Rev. Edward Lester of Immanuel Baptist Church, a few blocks from the proposed site, claimed to have seen a "great deal of animosity of people around the church." Claiming no prejudice, he hoped the city would change policy and "forestall possible overt action."[74]

The mayor explained, "We would have to break faith with all humanity if it were stopped. We cannot draw any line. We have to look at it as a humanitarian matter."[75]

Later, Ray Martinez was quoted on his disgust at the church's stand against integration. "I can't believe that any group or any man supposed to teach the teachings of the Lord could make such protests that tend to further discrimination and racial prejudices. Also this group is to be reminded that we just finished a war where we defeated a nation that believed in the principles of the super race."

Before nightfall, a mass protest of integration was planned for the following day on the campus of Garfield Elementary School.

That next evening, the protest begun with a change in tactics. With city officials plainly refusing to change their plan for limited integration of veteran's housing, Eddie Poole stepped up and spoke. "We don't hate anybody. We're not fighting Mexicans, or Spanish Americans, or any other race. We're fighting the type of shacks they're going to be building in our neighborhood. Just look at the lumber – they're fire hazards. They're not fit for dogs to live in."

The Garfield Association was to now target the temporary housing, sections of which had already begun to arrive by train from Washington and were being stacked next to the construction site.

Poole continued: "We believe we can kill this thing with signatures." The crowd surged forward to sign a petition that had been brought to the meeting. The petition cited the project's risk factors as: lower property values, depreciation of land, undesirable community, fire hazards, already noticeable depreciation of homes in the neighborhood as a result of the project, non-compliance with city building codes and a general undue burden on the community.

Poole asked for contributions to pay for the legal costs and further denied any racism behind their goals. He explained that several Spanish American families already lived in the area, were good neighbors and were at the event.

Ray Martinez stepped forward in an attempt to stop the flow of signatures that could threaten the building of the veterans' housing entirely. "I am an American. Mexicans are born across the border. I was born right down the street, attended this (Garfield) school, and was a member of the scout troop at the Garfield church. If you block this thing now, you are hurting every veteran. These homes will be better than living in tents. Please don't sign any petition that will keep your boys from having a home."

He recounted the temporary nature of the housing and explained that supplies were scarce. When he had finished, he was met with some applause. But before his words could sink in, Poole overpowered his point by reminding the crowd that this fight was about the quality of construction – not against the veterans.

The labor leader, John Dutch, again tried to voice his support of the integrated veterans' housing. But he and another speaker, future State Representative James Carreón, were quieted with shouts from the crowd as it pushed forward to continue signing the petitions.[77]

By week's end, on June 6, the newspaper announced that the city had voted unanimously to continue with the project. James Marsh of the Congress of Industrial Organizations, who introduced the resolution, said he was "bitterly opposed to racial discrimination in veterans' housing."

He continued: "The word is out that the housing project will be filled with a lot of zoot-suiters. That's hogwash."[78]

The FPHA (Federal Public Housing Administration) awarded a contract for more than $200,000 to the Dell E. Webb Construction Co. for reassembling the houses and connecting city utilities.[79]

This was one of many federal housing contracts to Del Webb that gave his company early success. It provided the experience that later led to the creation of Sun City, and a nationwide change in housing developments.

That day, concrete was poured for the foundation of the homes and ditches were dug for utilities to be laid. Promises were made to landscape the area and paint the houses. They hoped to be finished in August or September of that year.

The 4th of July was a relatively peaceful Thursday that led into a long, festive weekend. But Eddie Poole had not yet given up his fight. When Tuesday came, he marched in to file the signed petitions against the housing unit. He again explained that he'd been authorized to demand that the mayor and the commissioners post a bond swearing to the teardown of the project in two years.

Mayor Busey looked up, over his glasses, "No, I won't."

"When I assumed this office," Busey continued, "I raised my hand and took an oath to carry out my duties to the best of my ability. A bond wouldn't be any better than my word."[80]

The city had already signed a contract with the federal government. That was enough of an agreement for the mayor.

The Garfield Association would continue its protests through the following months. It brought a suit against the Public Housing Authority to stop the project. On numerous occasions, American Legion Thunderbird Post 41 would spar with Eddie Poole and the Garfield Property Owners Protective Association. Finally, on Dec. 11, 1946, the issue came before the Arizona Supreme Court.

And the court overturned the case. Integration of housing was to be upheld.

It took time, and numerous setbacks, but the 156-unit project was completed by the end of the year and opened in February 1947. Just 24 units were provided to Mexican Americans.

It was named the Harry Córdova Housing Project, in honor of a Mexican American Army corporal killed in the Battle of Normandy, June 1944. He was a member of the Army Medical Corps, and the brother of Luis Córdova, who had founded the Latino American Club in the 1930s.

The project operated for more than five years, closing in June 1952, soon after the landowners raised rental fees for the property. By then, 900 veterans and their families had used the frame houses to get on their feet.[81]

Throughout the late 1940s and into the 50s, Garfield then was taken over by Hispanic populations seeking to be closer to their friends and family, slowly pushing out the Anglos.

But this was a military housing project. There was a larger battle. The city itself was still segregated.

Covenant busting

"No lot or tract, or any part thereof, shall be leased, let, occupied, sold or transferred to anyone other than to members of the white or Caucasian race except those of Mexican or Spanish ancestry, and this exclusion shall include those having perceptible strains of Mexican, Spanish, Asiatic, negro or Indian blood."
                                        —Race restricting deed in Phoenix.

Life continued as usual beyond the curbs of veteran housing in Phoenix. Latinos were not welcome in the communities of Phoenix proper. Post 41 would again be called upon to fight for the rights to equal housing opportunities.

The great housing explosion of the Western U.S. was about to kick into overdrive and bring thousands of construction jobs.[82] A few hurdles had to be crossed first.

In 1947, a housing construction site was under development at 27th Avenue and Van Buren, just beyond the edge of Anglo tolerance of Latino homes. In 1947, Donald Gaylien walked in to the offices for a housing development called Melrose Manor on North 7th Avenue. He was a well-spoken professor at the American Institute of Foreign Trade. He had returned home after serving in the same naval aviation unit as a future president, George Bush Sr. He easily qualified to purchase a home. As he was prepared to sign papers, he began to speak to his wife in Spanish.[83]

That was a problem. His last name hadn't sounded Mexican. It wasn't until his use of Spanish that he was found to have "perceptible strains of Mexican blood." The professor was denied his home. Donald Gaylien was also a member of the American Legion Thunderbird Post 41.

After getting word of the incident, the post sent Ray Martinez to investigate. The following weeks would be a test of his patience and resolve.

One day, Ray used his lunch break from driving a city bus on the Duppa Villa route to visit the offices of Stewart Construction Co. to inquire about purchasing a home.

The man's response was not unexpected. "Well, we don't sell to Mexicans or greasers or ... what do you call 'em? What do you call yourselves?"

Ray was unfazed. "We call ourselves Americans."

The employee he'd approached continued. "Well, I don't know. They use this word about Mexicans and greasers and spics and you know. Well, anyway – we don't sell to you."

Ray Martinez walked out. But he returned the next day, much to the dismay of company officials. "So what the hell do you want?"

Ray's reply was succinct. "I want to speak to Mr. Stewart. He's the boss isn't he? Superintendent? The owner of the construction company? He's the developer. I wanna talk to him."

"Well he doesn't wanna talk to you."

Ray told the man, "Well fine, but I'll be here every day 'til he might change his mind."

And he was. He refused to give up. He'd survived worse in the barrios south of Phoenix.

Martinez described the price of patience in an interview years later. "So I'd go every day and then they'd come in and insult me or they came out and spilled water on me and whatever, you know? A lot of indignities and all that.[84]

"One day they decided they had had enough of his visits. "We're goddamned sick and tired of you, Mexican."

He reminded them, "You're in here selling to the public. I'm the public and I'm here to inquire."

Irritated, one man offered a compromise. "If Mr. Stewart will talk to you, will you stop coming?"

"Absolutely." Ray left the office with an appointment set

Post 41 marches in the 1948 Memorial Day Parade.

PHOTO COURTESY OF AMERICAN LEGION POST 41

for the following Tuesday at 1:30 p.m.

When Tuesday came Ray returned to meet with the owner. As he arrived, one of the sales managers walked up to him and pointed as he spoke. "Go into Mr. Stewart's office, there. There's a secretary."

As he entered the elusive businessman's office, a secretary rose from her desk. Turning to him she spoke measured and with indignation. "I want you to know one thing. Mr. Stewart is not going to meet with you today, nor any other day. So the best thing you can do is just get the *hell* out of here, and *stay* out of here."

The commander of Post 41 was not swayed. "Miss," He began, "I want you to give Mr. Stewart a message.

"You tell Mr. Stewart that he's using federal money on FHA housing and that the Arizona Bank is providing the money and that I have the money to go to court as early as this next week and we're going to place an injunction on the money and on this construction job. We're gonna bring it to a halt. Because you cannot discriminate if you're using federal money. Against us, as Hispanics, you cannot discriminate."

Ray drove his point home even further. "Now you tell Mr. Stewart that we have our attorneys ready to go and all they're waiting for … is to hear the results of this meeting and I'm going to say, 'Go.'" (Red Harkins had again donated the money to cover court costs).

"So you say Mr. Stewart doesn't wanna meet with me. I said he will meet me. Possibly as early as next week, but it'll be in court … he will meet me."

With that, Ray left.

After his workday was over, Ray headed home. His flustered wife caught his attention immediately.

"There's some guy name of Stewart's been calling since 4 o'clock this afternoon. Every 10 minutes and I keep telling him you won't be here 'til 7!"

Ray was not surprised. "I know what he wants."

A mere five minutes passed before phone rang again. Mr. Jack Stewart began speaking immediately.

"Ray. I wanna tell you how sorry I am that I wasn't there to meet with you this afternoon."

"Well, this is the message I got when I went to your office."

Stewart was animated in his response. "By golly! They got it all screwed up because I said no such a thing!" There was a pause, then, "Well, listen. You can come out tomorrow. We are selling to any Hispanic that comes up here and just tell 'em come tomorrow and they'll be attended to and they'll be attended to *right away.*"

Ray wasn't satisfied with just this, nor did he want to risk another refusal to any Hispanic wanting to buy a home. He explained, "All that we want to do is just settle this peacefully but these are the conditions I'm going to set today, in a friendly way.

"Now you probably belong to the homebuilders association. Well now you tell them, the next time, we don't have the patience.

"If they fail to sell to *one* Hispanic we shall be in court the following day. You tell 'em that, and anybody in the future. If there's any discrimination, we are not going to negotiate. We are not going and see you or try to see you.

We shall file and tie up your money and try to get you disqualified from these federal FHA funds.

"Can you do that?"

"Mr. Martinez. I will do that."[85]

The success of the Harry Córdova Project and overcoming the Stewart Construction Co. would give Post 41 the boldness to send a letter petitioning the Executive Director of Public Housing Earl Schnurr to issue an order desegregating the Marcos de Niza Housing Project, managed by Post 41 member Ray Yanez, and opened in 1941.[86]

The 1948 court case Shelley v. Kraemer would go one step further by prohibiting the enforcement of racially restrictive housing covenants across the nation. But old habits die hard. Realtors and subdivision salesmen continued to refuse Hispanics seeking to buy homes. The battle was far from over. This can be seen in the story of Lincoln and Eleanor Ragsdale's determination to buy in the Encanto District of central Phoenix in the 1950s[87]

Building a home

A year and a half of Tuesday meetings at the restaurant had passed. The post's membership had swelled to 300. They had become involved in numerous events and functions. It was time for a new home.

Soon after its founding, Post 41 members began the long search for a new home. A piece of vacant land at 2nd Avenue and Grant Street, south of Van Buren, seemed perfect. It was across from Grant Park, a popular Latino hangout and the site of many of Post 41's events. But the lot belonged to the City of Phoenix Parks Dept. The men lobbied the city, wading through red tape for nearly a year before receiving permission from the parks department and the city commission to construct their building there.[88]

Pipa Fuentes with wheel barrow and Ray Martinez with shovel, helping the men build Post 41

PHOTO COURTESY OF THE CHICANO COLLECTION, DEPARTMENT OF ARCHIVES AND SPECIAL COLLECTIONS, ARIZONA STATE UNIVERSITY

Post members worked with the city to iron out a lease agreement at $1 per year for 50 years, with no property taxes. Barry Goldwater was beginning to have pull in local politics, and lent a hand in convincing the city.[89] Part of the agreement was the maintenance of an old adobe structure, the Darrel Duppa Building built in the 1870s on the south end of the lot. It sat derelict and unused for decades.

With the lease signed, the veterans immediately began calling on post members and the community for help. Originally they had hoped to obtain a surplus building from one of the state army camps. Frank Fuentes and Ray

Martinez drove as fast as they could to purchase a structure. Marana. Coolidge. Florence. Douglas. Everywhere. Sometimes they didn't show in time, or they found the structure too inadequate for their needs.

As they frantically sought a surplus building, one member spotted articles about legionnaires cooperating to build homes for each other in the housing crunch that had yet to be solved. The idea was brought up at a Tuesday meeting and soon the surplus building hunt was dropped in favor of building their own. They began to raise funds, secure building materials and gather volunteers to help build their home.[90]

They broke ground on July 26, 1947. The men were often rewarded after hot, dusty days of construction with kegs of beer. The post hired only those who were necessary if a task required skills or tools that the community didn't already possess. Steadily the new building arose as more members joined in. Florencio "Lencho" Othon remembers. "I didn't get involved in it right at the very beginning, but after about two months of going down there and seeing all the work, I got involved in it, too."[91]

Through the summer months and into the winter, the men pushed on. Often they held post meetings on the construction site, "under the stars, under an open sky."[92] Sometimes they ran out of money. A barbecue, festival, bingo parties or dances helped to provide additional funds.[93]

Then, in March 1948, their new home was complete. They had spent $10,000 for a building valued at $60,000. The local newspaper ran a small article announcing the dedication ceremony and commended the "resolute way the post members had tackled a job for which they had only $2,700 when they started out. All the time the post was working on this building project, it was carrying out the sponsorship of a Boy Scout troop, a Class A junior basketball team, maintaining a blood bank and backing the championship team of the Phoenix Gazette Golden Gloves state-wide boxing tournament."[94]

The newspaper had announced that Ira Hayes, the famed Pima Indian who'd help raise a flag at Iwo Jima, would be on hand to raise the post's flag. After Mass at Immaculate Heart, the community surrounded a temporary

Raising the flag on dedication day for Post 41, March 14, 1948

American Legion
Thunderbird Post 41

★ DEDICATION SOUVENIR ★

March 14, 1948–Phoenix, Arizona

IMAGE COURTESY OF AMERICAN LEGION POST 41

Dedication booklet showing the original Post 41 of 1948. In 1949 there would be a new addition. The Ronda Room was added in 1957. And another addition would come after that.

stage at the post. Pipa Fuentes presided over the two-hour ceremony, handing out 75 citations as he rattled off numerous thank-you's to those in the community who had helped build their home.

Fuentes seemed to know every individual involved. A Mr. Cruz and Mr. Dominguez had laid block, half of which was donated by Thomas Brothers Superlite Block Manufacturers. A Mr. Chavez and Mr. Johnson had pitched in as carpenters. Ted Olea put down the plumbing, with parts donated by John H. Welch Plumbing.

No four-star generals were present. The color guard marched the flags in precision. The crowd watched as post members grabbed a rope and raised the building's first flag. People laughed at rough jokes and smiled in the achievement. There had been no waiting for help. They had done it; built their own home.[95]

Years later, Barry Goldwater reminisced about the dedication ceremony for the humble building.

"Judged through sophisticated eyes of most of my friends, the building would have provoked no great admiration. But those of us present actually relived the loving construction block by block and timber by timber, for this building, built in an area of our city which the federal planners would call underprivileged, was constructed not of concrete and mortar but of love and devotion and determination."

The March 14 dedication booklet that was printed for the ceremony includes a quote, which now adorns the side of the building:

"Ever since it can be remembered, Americans of Spanish speaking ancestry have striven to promote the welfare of our country to uphold and defend its constitution and to fight for it proudly in time of war. It is not intended to drop the battle of justice, freedom and democracy merely because the sound of gunfire has stilled."

At its completion the building was the result of more than $50,000 invested. And it had been built just in time. Soon after the post became a gathering point for the community. It was a venue for regular dances, wedding receptions, Boy Scout meetings and activist meetings – community functions that continue to the present day.[97]

Within three years the post's membership roll would grow to 900, and two more additions would grace the post.

Community action and the better halves

On Dec. 19, 1947, the post held a meeting. Members were surrounded by mothers, sisters and wives. Ray Martinez and Frank Fuentes proposed the formation of a women's auxiliary to Post 41. The vote was unanimous.

That night, 30 women joined.

Anita Lewis, just 23 years old, was elected the first president. The women's auxiliary from the Luke-Greenway post helped them organize and soon the Post 41 group was self-sufficient.

The women planned whatever the men neglected to give attention to. They organized dances and holiday events. Some cooked meals for the meetings or community events. Others decorated the hall or chaperoned events. One member, Bertha Enriquez, volunteered as a chaperone for Grant Park's Campfire Girls. Other auxiliary members drove girls to softball games.[98]

Post member Tony Valenzuela remembers how Pipa and the auxiliary members made construction of their building bearable. "We'd all work to maybe 2 o'clock, and then the auxiliary would feed us. They would do the cooking. And then Frank Fuentes would open up a great big tub of cold beer and we'd have a ball. You know, that was great! Especially on weekends. The auxiliary's always been good and we never give them credit."[99]

But the auxiliary's contributions would grow to be much more than simply day-to-day activities. They often took to the streets, much like the CSO in Los Angeles, gathering signatures from the community for election issues and bonds during the day while the men worked. In the evening the men would assume those duties.

The post also gave support during the more difficult moments of community life. It was not uncommon for Ray Martinez to get a phone call from Frank Fuentes that somebody needed to come down to the Post; Ira Hayes had come into town again, drowning his demons in alcohol. Ray would drive Ira back home to the reservation in Sacaton.

Melancholy touched them all in April 1949, soon after they had built their new home. Raymond N. Moraga finally came home. He had died on a flight mission over Normandy four days after D-Day. It had taken four years for his family to bring him home from Europe. Post 41 was on hand for the funeral ceremonies that Saturday morning.[100]

Honoring the dead was not the only heartbreak for Post 41. Newborn babies did not receive the care they needed. Mothers could not get the education they needed to be good mothers, nor find easy resources to care for their children.

Post 41 women's auxiliary in 1948

Father Emmett McLoughlin had done immense good for South Phoenix. He fought for the Mexican American and African American communities when nobody else seemed to care. One of his lasting efforts would be the creation of a maternity clinic in an old barber shop in 1943. The clinic would grow into the St. Monica Hospital, later renamed Memorial Hospital. But, in the clinic's earliest days, it was not enough.

The year 1949 was difficult. Several babies in the barrios had died. Families pleaded for help.

To battle the health-care deficiency in Latino communities, Post 41 took action. With funds raised at a Friday night benefit dance on Dec. 1, 1949, Post 41 swiftly organized a health clinic to help new mothers. On Dec. 6 the Well-Baby Clinic opened in an old army barracks building next to the post. It was immediately filled with 120 babies and their worried mothers.

Lencho Othon remembers the short lifespan of the clinic. "We had some nurses that volunteered their time, on the weekends especially. Doctors, same way, they would come over on the weekends, work with the nurses here. And then if I remember right, we had one girl that would be here most of the week for working mothers that would come over ... with their younger kids."[101]

The clinic would remain open until 1950, when services improved and were more available. But before the clinic doors closed, the national office of the legion sent a doctor to Phoenix to issue a citation to Post 41 for its outstanding contribution in improved services to children's health.[102]

Opening our own eyes

Another of Post 41's goals was to raise national attention to the local issues of the Salt River Valley.

As the post was being built in 1947, another organization was coming to life in Los Angeles. The Community Service Organization (CSO) was founded by Antonio Rios, Edward R. Roybal and Fred Ross Sr. to combat community issues, ranging from education to police abuse and discrimination. The CSO would train some of the iconic leaders of the Chicano movement who would rise to prominence throughout the 1960s and 1970s – César Chávez, Dolores Huerta and Gilbert Padilla.

Within two years of its start, the CSO was succeeding in voter registration drives throughout Los Angeles. In 1949, its effort produced 15,000 new voters – most of whom helped elect CSO co-founder Edward Roybal, as Los Angeles' first Hispanic city council member in 65 years. They were soon expanding their efforts throughout the Southwestern U.S.

Lito Peña remembers Post 41 lending barracks to the CSO in hopes of finding the same success in Phoenix. "We had an organization that we were trying to build up voting strength in the Chicano community. And I wrote a letter to one outfit and they wrote back to me and said, 'Write to Fred Ross.' And oh, there was another fellow, Saul Alinsky. Said, 'Write to Saul Alinsky and tell him what your problem is.' And so I did. And in a few days, Fred Ross came by, talked and I took him on a tour through the schools. And that's how we got involved with CSO."

As a CSO worker, Peña fought to improve unsanitary conditions in the barrios by having more frequent trash pickups, cleaning up alleys and covering exposed city sewers.

Whenever a political issue was deemed important to Post 41, members would appear at government meetings and fill the rooms. If necessary, they mobilized their community. One such example was a 1948 attempt to allocate some of the local levy taxes to improve several schools attended by Mexican American children.

The voter registration experiences of the CSO in Los Angeles and LULAC Ladies Councils in El Paso showed what was possible. Following their example, the members of Post 41 took to the streets when the city council told them that a bond issue vote was necessary to authorize use of the funds for these schools.

The Post 41 Women's Auxiliary canvassed during the day, while their husbands worked, and the men helped during the evening. When their first attempt failed, they tried again. Within a year, the bond issue was passed and their schools received facility upgrades.

In the late 1940s, another bond issue was up for vote on providing improvement funds to Grant, Central and Harmon parks in South Phoenix. Again the women's auxiliary took to the streets and residents voted to appropriate $365,000 for the parks.[103]

The new Post 41 building fills for its dedication dinner in 1948.

Ray Martinez speaks with Arizona Gov. Ernest W. McFarland (1955-1959), center, and his associate.

1950s

No war should be forgotten

As World War II began to fall into the history books, a Korean conflict sprang from its ashes. The U.S. was shifting its focus onto a bitter division in Asia and the threat of a red Russia. Affected was the political scene of the 1950s.

From 1945 to 1950, the Soviet Union and the U.S. were in a stalemate over hemispheric dominance and anti-Communism. Korea was at its center, literally and figuratively, bisected on maps by the 38th parallel. The north half of the country began to organize a militia, with the Soviets whispering in their ears and selling it arms. In the South, the U.S. struggled with weak forces and a populace that wasn't fond of them as the occupying force that had replaced Japanese domination. The country was cracking.

As the new decade started, Henry Daley Jr. was still a high school sophomore at Phoenix Technical School. After his basketball team played the season's last game, Henry and a few friends decided to drop out of school. They were going to enlist in the military. It seemed like something fun to do. So young Henry filled out his paperwork and brought it home for his parents to sign. It wasn't an easy task.

His mother was not happy. World War II had just ended. She'd been through the agony of her husband landing at Normandy and battling across Europe. He was captured during the Battle of the Bulge and became a POW. He had made it home. Her brother was not as lucky.

But her husband stood up for his son's decision. "You're missin' a lot of school." He turned to her, "The Army will make a man out of him."

Eventually they signed the papers. During the discussion, it had never crossed either parent's mind that Henry Daley Jr. was 16. He had changed his birthday to be accepted legally into the Army. Recruiters didn't seem to take notice, either.

On June 25, 1950, two months after Daley had finished his basic training and was accepted to a clerical school, Korea found itself ripping apart at the seams. North Korea, with Soviet resources, invaded the southern half. Two days later President Truman ordered air and sea support for South Korea.

In mid-November 1950 Gen. MacArthur was on a flight home. He turned to two generals seated with him, to remark, "You tell the boys that when they get to the Yalu (River) they are going home. I want to make good on my statement that they are going to eat Christmas dinner at home."[1]

At the start of the war, Daley was one of about 20,000 Hispanics serving in the armed forces. Within three years that number would swell to almost 148,000 Hispanic volunteers or draftees. Most would serve in the Army and Marine Corps. One largely Hispanic group was Charlie Company of the 13th

Infantry Battalion in Tucson. Its men were from Arizona, Texas, New Mexico and California. Daley, though, was not with them on the front lines.

But his dream of joining them there was not so easy. He wanted to be an infantryman, just as his father. Before the U.S. entered Korea, he had already been put in a clerical school. He applied to transfer to the infantry, but was not accepted. He tried again and again. Eventually, his persistence convinced the Army to transfer him into the 25th Infantry Division in March 1953 after a short return to boot camp.

The delay may have saved him from one of the Korean War's tragedies.

All soldiers battle unseen dangers, sometimes deadly and sometimes haunting survivors across a lifetime. Soldiers in World War I were decimated by the 1918 influenza pandemic. Many Vietnam veterans came home carrying the hidden effects of Agent Orange. Desert Storm veterans struggled to gain attention and support for the little-known Gulf War syndrome.

In Korea, the men were caught in the jaws of a brutal winter. By December, MacArthur was battling criticism for thinking the war would be swift and that the boys would be home by Christmas. This comment was tragically tied to the decision not to send the men into Korea with winter gear. At night the soldiers huddled together, trying to fight off the dull pain of frostbite as the mercury was in freefall to minus-30 degrees.

When Daley stepped foot in Korea, the weather had improved only slightly. "To me the worst part was the winters there. I got there in March and it was very, very cold at the time.

United States Marines drive forward after effective close air support of F4U-5 Corsairs. Billows of smoke and flame from a small target area bear out the accuracy of the flying Leathernecks' marksmanship.

PHOTO RELEASED TO PUBLIC. HM-SN-98-06704

"We just had World War II equipment. By that time, they had these boots that they had come out with, so I was wearing those but it was still cold.

"I had a lot of trouble with my feet. They turned sort of a grayish blackish color. I told a medic about it. He wrapped my feet up with a lot of bandage, and they started swelling up. And so I just took them off. But I never went to see a ... I never went on sick call for this reason. We'd never go on sick call, you know." Then Daley mumbles something about the risk of getting ribbed for not being macho.

But there were also moments of warmth and satisfaction. Of all places, it was on the front lines in Korea that young Daley saw a chance to finally get his high school diploma. The Army was offering G.E.D. tests. The company commander had asked one day if any of the soldiers wanted to take a shot at it.

Daley spoke up. "Yeah, I wanna try it. It's my last chance."

Five men joined him, and they were brought back to the reserves at the rear. Food was served. Beers were cracked open, and the men shook off the cold, hoping to forget their worries.

"I was the only one that passed the test. Now, some of those guys had three years high school. Not that I was smarter than them. They went through it just to relax and get something to drink and just get off the front line. That was the only reason. For once, I took something serious. And I went through it and I got my G.E.D."

Post member Tony Valenzuela remembered that following his friend into the service would take him to the Korean War,

"I came to ASU in 1948, that was before the Korean War.... I had two years of college, started my third year. And one of my best buddies, he wasn't cuttin' it. He decided he was gonna quit and go in the Air Force. I said, 'Nooo! What the hell you gonna...' He said, 'I already enlisted.'"

Two weeks later Valenzuela enlisted in the Air Force. He trained as an electronics specialist, repairing aircraft equipment and occasionally testing it while the pilot took the plane up into the clouds. It was job that would take him some place he hadn't expected when the base loudspeaker called out his name.

"Sgt. Valenzuela. Show up at Ops with your gear."

Valenzuela quickly walked into the operations area reporting for duty. The commanding officer spoke. "You're going on a mission." Valenzuela had never trained as a pilot, but he knew the equipment, and that was enough.

Valenzuela accepted his new role. "Holy Christ! So I did. I made several (missions). Never scared the hell out of me at all. It was an adventure! We'd go out. Five or six of us go... three of us come back."

In July word came that a cease-fire agreement was about to be signed. Henry Daley would always remember the day. "It was my wife's birthday. Well it was my girlfriend's birthday then. It ended on July 27. So I remember it for that day and everything. Of course at the same time you were happy to hear that the war was over."

Three months later, 20-year-old Henry Daley Jr. arrived in California. In a hurry to get home, he took a plane to Phoenix. He saw no ticker-tape parades. No celebrity veterans were honored for their impossible tales of bravery. "Coming home at that time during the Korean War, there was no fanfare going or leaving, like there is now. You just came home. Nobody noticing – other than your family.

"Nobody even knew you were gone. ... There was hardly anything in the papers. There was nothing on TV about the war. I just noticed there was no response. No emotion. No nothing by the people. It was just somewhere you went and then came back. The people who served and were involved in it and had family, and those were the ones that knew about it. It really is a forgotten war. To this day I still feel that way."2

The Korean War would, indeed, be largely forgotten between those of World War II and Vietnam. During the Korean War, nine Hispanics would receive the Medal of Honor and more than 100 more received Distinguished Service Crosses and Silver Stars for their bravery in combat.

Two days after Henry Daley, Jr. came home, there was a knock at his door. Pipa Fuentes had come to sign Daley up as a Post 41 member, and refusal was not an option. "Here's your card. Now sign it, and give me $2."

A veteran in every house

The tall, imposing rebel priest, Father Albert Braun, had survived numerous Japanese prison camps and was freed by American forces on Aug. 29, 1945, after the atomic bomb ended the war. He returned to the U.S., gaunt and tired. New aches spread through his aging legs. After visiting his former congregation, the Mescalaro Apaches of New Mexico, Braun took one final military assignment in Hawaii before retiring from the Army. It was 1949. He was as strong-willed and stubborn as ever.

The Catholic Church sent Braun to Phoenix. He took a teaching job at St. Mary's High School. He soon quit so he could minister to barrios in South Phoenix, more specifically the Golden Gate community.

When Braun came to South Phoenix, he found a community of aging houses with dirt floors lining dusty roads. Some families pulled water from old wells. No street lights graced the skies and no sewers ran underground. Contamination of the land was tragic, made worse by the industrial centers surrounding the neighborhoods and the city storm drains that had spewed storm water and untreated sewage into South Phoenix since the 1890s.[3]

In 1952, the closest church was Immaculate Heart of Mary on 9th Street and Washington. Built in 1928 after the community had been forced to worship in the basement of St. Mary's church, it was the first church built before the turn of the 20th century. But Golden Gate needed its own house of worship. Many residents had no car and there was no bus service to much of South Phoenix.

When Braun began his Sunday sermons, they were under a makeshift ramada. His weathered face showed every bit of his 65 rugged years in the dry air. He read bible passages under the thatched roof of brittle palm fronds as people fanned themselves with Bibles and empty hands. It was as elegant a church as the barrio could afford.

The congregation was slow to accept him. But when he proposed they build their own church, their skeptical faces lit with interest. For Father Braun, it was not a new proposal. Thirty years before he had helped the Mescalero Apaches in New Mexico build a church with only the materials of the

Father Albert Braun gives an outdoor Mass to a congregation in South Phoenix.

area. Soon he was raising churches and eyebrows in South Phoenix.

Over the next two years, Golden Gate residents met Braun's challenge and the walls of Sacred Heart Church rose. In April 1954, the first baptism was held before the roof had been raised. Along the way, Braun secretly set aside bricks to build a parochial school. When the school's construction was done, he joyously announced its completion to the Catholic Diocese. Despite the surprise and displeasure of diocesan officials, this defiant man of God didn't stop there.

His involvement in the community was local legend. He was not afraid to get down into the dirt with his congregation. If a wife needed her drunk husband at home, Father Braun walked into the bar and dragged the man out.

He smuggled stolen goods back into the stores they were lifted from to save a young sinner from his crime. With smiles, community members remember the night a gang hung out near his chapel. Through the night they made noise, despite his verbal warnings to stop. Not one to shy away from confrontation, he stepped into the fray, tightened his fists and swung. The gang dispersed.[4]

By the time his health forced him to retire in 1962, Braun had founded three more chapels. He coerced the city into paving roads, building sidewalks, providing gas and adding a sewer system. He had even served on the Governor's Narcotics Study Committee. Crime dropped, pride lifted and seeds of a real community were sown.

But how does one man achieve this? Certainly not through his efforts alone. No individual is wholly responsible for this mid-century barrio renaissance of Phoenix, any more than Rembrandt or Da Vinci could ever be called the driving force of the European Renaissance.

Braun would go door to door and bring people to church. He knew most every household and had eaten dinner with many of them. With such a connection, he found many veterans sitting at those dinner tables. The veteran chaplain of two world wars saw immediately that almost every house in Phoenix had a veteran of the last war. Here was a connection that could be nurtured. The priest joined Post 41 and the legend grew bigger.[5]

Before long, Father Braun could be found at Post 41 most evenings, draining more than a few glasses of beer with his fellow veterans after a day of fighting for his community's needs. Barry Goldwater was one of those fights. It was not uncommon to hear the two clash at city council meetings in a bout of colorful language.

In the late 1950s, Goldwater stepped into the post and walked briskly up to the Ronda Room bar. He had just come from city hall where he had been verbally ripped apart by Braun, who was demanding amenities for his community. Goldwater slid onto a bar stool. "I sure need a good strong drink. That Father Albert Braun just damn near ripped me apart!"

A shot of whiskey was set in front of him.

Then the room brightened with sunlight as the front door opened. Looking up, Goldwater saw the good father walk in. Not wanting to suffer more, he slid his drink off the bar and attempted to head for a dark corner.

"Barry, I saw you!" the priest bellowed. "You know what? I'm gonna have one, too."

Whether the future senator wanted company or not, Braun joined the politician. They traded shots of whiskey through the night, and out of arguments, a friendship was born.

Many a night, joined by Pipa and others, the men could be seen in a dark corner, talking politics, arguing about the community's needs, fighting over the value of worker's unions or laughing at jokes as they lifted another glass. It was here that Braun was known to whisper – and often yell – his community's needs into the ears of men who could do something about it.

With a commanding priest and respected politician at its side, Post 41 had become well-connected to the city's heartbeat. With close-knit friendships among the veterans, the church, activists and families, the barrio was pulling itself up and out of the dust. Communities that always had to provide for themselves now began to assert themselves. At last the barrios of South Phoenix were becoming a unified community and tearing down segregation.

Thunderbird Post 41 was also gaining national attention as one of the better known American Legion posts. By 1954, Ray Martinez had served as commander of the American Legion Department of Arizona and been named as the national representative of the American Legion Child Welfare Program.[6] That year, Ray would even make a bid to the state senate.

A 1954 business card promoting Ray Martinez as state senator.

When he failed to win the election, he decided he'd rather help others, and not run for office again. His daugher, Norma Keirmeyr, remembers one of her father's quips, "If dogs and kids could vote, I'd be president."

The post was becoming a voting force of which the new charter government had noticed. With help, of course, from Barry Goldwater. He had asked Ray Martinez for advice on winning the Hispanic vote if he should run for office. Ray told Goldwater that if he joined Post 41, he would have that vote. Goldwater's growing affection for the Mexican American post would soon lead to an honorary lifetime membership bestowed on him, whether he wanted it or not.

During a 2006 interview, Lencho Othon remembered the events surrounding the honor. Goldwater was persistent about refusing to be repaid for money he'd given the post.

> "He used to come down and walk around, look around and do things for the post. As a matter of fact, when we were building a second addition to the post, Barry loaned us ... he gave us, I think it was about $3,500, which was a heck of a lot of money at that time for the refrigeration unit we wanted to put in there. We didn't have the money. So he gave us a check for $3,500 so that we would continue with the project. Later on I started a bingo program with the intent of making enough money to pay back Barry Goldwater – which we did, after a year or two.....
>
> "He became a life member a little bit later because at that time we presented a check to him, and .... he said, we didn't give you a loan. He says 'that was our contribution to the post.' So he wouldn't accept the check. So I told his wife that it will make the boys feel better if he would accept it. But Barry go ahead and take the check. Right about that time he was made a life member of the post.
>
> "But about a couple of weeks later, we got a check in the mail for, I think it was close to $3,500 or something like that as a donation. So what are you going to do?"[7]

Ray Martinez with daughter Norma, 1948

Barry's wife had sent the money back. The post decided to make him an honorary member. It was all it could do.

Goldwater had certainly earned the honor for his support and for the many nights of camaraderie drinking with his post friends. He also gave them an ear and an in-road to the political halls of Phoenix. But as Barry Goldwater's political star continued to rise, he decided to run for the U.S. Senate and those friendships became more distant. Soon enough, though, more of them would find themselves decision-makers in those same halls.

The failure of commission

Politics were not only changing nationally. There would also be a political shift in Phoenix, and Post 41 found itself involved with the city's inner workings.

In its earliest years, Phoenix had been a mayor/city council system. In August 1913, this changed to a city manager/city commission system. Unlike the old process that elected representatives from each of its wards, the new commission members would from then on be elected "at-large."

This effectively robbed poorer wards of any say in city decisions, a result that was acknowledged and desired by defenders of the new system. As secretary of the Phoenix Good Government League, R.L. Dyer noted at a meeting in February 1914, "The Third and Fourth wards (both in South Phoenix) are composed of people who do not meet the high ideals of those here present."[8]

Throughout the 1930s and well into the 1940s, Phoenix politics slipped quietly into corruption: "the home of some of the wildest political manipulations imaginable, a curious combination of big city bossism and old west frontierism."[9] With World War II, then the return of soldiers and loss of military work contracts, the city seemed in a constant shifting confusion. Local government struggled to keep up with the needs, services, changing factions and backroom deals that plagued it daily.

With Democrats in complete power during the 1940s, they became the "force to copy." Alliances were made with the party, regardless of one's difference in political beliefs. These connections were in turn used to secure elections and legislation that met their needs – with the freedom of a non-partisan election system.

But by 1945, Phoenix had become mired in its political disasters, prostitution rings, union strikes and deteriorating slums. The at-large system had fallen far short of the lofty ideals Phoenix needed as it grew. Its supporters committed the sorts of sins they had suggested only the impoverished southern half of town would create.

With the end of World War II, veterans returned to the Valley, and war-time workers settled into new jobs in the growing city. Its population began a sharp growth. John F. Long and Del Webb, who had started his business with government construction contracts such as the Harry S. Córdova project, were now building a new housing trend. Their ideas would soon create a nation of suburbia and urban sprawl. And, as a baby boom generation began to take its first steps, the homes were being filled as fast as they were built.

To politicians, this population growth translated into something simple: thousands of new voters. In Phoenix, a new elite coalition, called the Charter Government Committee, would be formed of conservative Democrats and the growing Republican Party. At the start of the 1950s this group was poised to take advantage of the blundering city government, to seize control and right their sinking ship. Through this storm of political and cultural activity, several Latino leaders would find their way into power. Just as Danny Rodriguez had told his niece by Tempe Beach Pool, times were indeed changing.

A change of politics

In 1946, a new man was put in charge of the city of Phoenix, Mayor Ray Busey. The following year he announced a plan to revise the city's charter, as he strongly opposed the non-partisan politics that had become the norm in Phoenix. His plan would eliminate the at-large election system that had excluded poorer regions three decades before. This unpopular change upset many politicians, and they united against him almost as soon as he had been elected. Mayor Busey was quickly left out of the city's loop, in a political freefall, made easier when he became sick and recovered at home from an operation.[10]

But before Busey fell entirely out of power, he struck back by creating the Charter Government Committee (CGC) to study city government and suggest charter revisions and reforms so his goals could be realized. Forty prominent citizens were asked to join the committee. One was a prominent businessman and veteran from South Phoenix: Barry Goldwater.

Goldwater had grown up in South Phoenix, the son of a well-known local mercantile family. The future Sky Harbor Airport was a cabbage field he would land on while teaching himself to fly shaky, primitive airplanes. By the late 1940s, he was one of Arizona's most celebrated pilots, along with Frank Luke. But in 1948, with the creation of the CGC, he was willingly thrust into local politics.[11]

Mayor Busey had set the stage but his creation, the CGC, had a mind of its own. Busey found the CGC quickly serving its own desires. Ray Busey lost the 1948 election to Nicholas Udall, a member of the CGC, who had run his campaign on claims he would restore the city to political calm waters. Once in office, Udall unwisely resigned from the CGC and quickly found the committee uncontrollable as well.

Unfettered, the Charter Government Committee plugged away at its work, as the new mayor found his control of city politics bogged down by the same back-door deals gone bad and political backstabbing that had plagued Busey.

In February 1951, sensing they could take control of the city, 30 of the original CGC members began planning their own vision of the future. For several months, they plotted a re-election strategy that would include showing their opponents links to the sinister politics of the 1930s and 40s, but also showing the modern successes of the city council.

To appeal to the voting public, they attempted to seed the city council with nominees that could be seen as every-men, and not elite businessmen. Their star nominee was E.H. Braatelien, a member of the local plumber's union. He felt that Phoenix was "being ruled and dictated to by people from the Country Club." The opposition responded in kind, when men such as Gus Rodriguez, a native of Mexico, and auto body shop owner, ran for office; and Charles Romaine, a retired railroad conductor and security guard.

The CGC's effort had nose-dived miserably; it lost in a 4-to-1 landslide.

Then, in the blur of one year, three of the most prominent charter office holders resigned – Mayor Udall, Harry Rosenszweig and Barry Goldwater, who had decided to run for the senate. Jack Williams was selected. The Charter Government Committee swiftly retooled its plan and decided to try again in the summer of 1953.

The CGC, a predictably white elite selected by Mayor Busey, decided to break new ground and broaden the "every-man" tactic. It made a bold move across ethnic boundaries, and asked Adam Diaz to try his hand at campaigning.

First Hispanic council member

W hen Adam Diaz was 14 and about to enter high school, his father died. His mother had weathered riots, Mexican rebellions and the bullets of Porfirio Diaz with her husband in 1906. She had managed to escape to Flagstaff and have her first child with him in 1909, young Adam. But now, she had to survive alone with five children and no money. She had helped raise money by selling enchiladas and tamales to build the new Immaculate Heart of Mary Church. But raising a family was different. So Adam left behind his education and found a job delivering messages and medicine by bicycle – at a nickel per delivery.

The following year, after a brief time delivering messages for Western Union, he became an elevator operator at the new Luhrs Building. The faces of white politicians and businessmen would pass him every day, heading to and from the meetings that made Phoenix. After Adam took a few accounting classes at a business school, George Luhrs offered him a job as a building manager and bookkeeper. Diaz found himself talking to these prominent personalities in the hotel's club, and he slowly became one of George Luhrs' most favored and dependable employees.

In 1929, Diaz stood facing his bride, Feliz, under the roof of the church his mother's tamales had helped build. Flush with the possibilities of a new life together, they bought a new home at 25th Street and Monte Vista Road. But when community Anglos harrassed Diaz and his new family, Feliz asked that they move for the safety of their children. They moved to Grant Park. He already had the memories of being forced to take his first holy communion in the basement of St. Mary's church while he heard the excitement and music as Anglo children celebrated above.

Adam might have stayed in the neighborhood, but his wife was not willing to risk life in a place they weren't welcome. They moved into the Grant Park neighborhood. As a teen pedaling messages around town, he had seen the lush green lawns and beautiful suburbs. Now he found he wasn't welcome to enjoy them for himself.

With the fire of his parents' revolution in his blood and the taste of segregation on his lips, he became active in his new community. From 1930

Adam Diaz with his family in the 1950s.

on, Diaz was intricately involved with local Mexican American organizations. He also fought to bring improvements to his barrio, improve education and help provide jobs.

During World War II, Diaz saw many of his neighbors from the south barrios of Phoenix in the Luhrs Building. As a member of the Arizona National Guard, he assumed he would be sent to fight after Pearl Harbor. But he was spared from the battlefield and given the task of recruiting young soldiers. He oversaw the largest induction center, set up downtown in the Luhrs Building. It was close enough for Latinos to enlist without venturing into the north half of the city.

With the end of World War II, Diaz stepped in to help an organization that had been close to his heart since its earliest days. In 1925, while delivering messages around town on his bicycle, a 14-year-old Adam Diaz saw a different world, north of Van Buren. Neighborhoods spread out before him into manicured lawns with fancy cars and clean streets. He dreamed of this new life.

There was one place that helped Latinos improve their lives; the Friendly House. Between deliveries, Adam pedaled off in search of the Friendly House. Soon he was walking up the sagging steps of a worn out old home and through the front door. He wanted advice on finding better employment.

"And I remember what Mrs. Green told me. She said immigrants needed to know how to make their own living. Learn to do a job that would keep them off the welfare cycle."[12]

More than 20 years later he took over the board of Friendly House. In 1949, the building had not improved. Faced with a leaky roof and a building that was falling apart, Diaz acted quickly. He approached New York Giants owner Horace Stoneham and suggested a benefit baseball game to help Friendly House.

Stoneham was impressed with the idea, but Diaz had to provide the other team. With the help of ballplayer Marin "Mike" de la Fuente, he "scrounged the best players Mexico had and the game was a sell-out."

On hand were the St. Mary's High school band and the Post 41 color guard. Luke-Greenway Post 1 arrived with its drum and bugle corps, and from Nogales came a singing trio and a mariachi band. Both Mayor Nicholas Udall and and Gov. Dan Garvey were joined by the Mexican Consul, Jesus Franco.

The exhibition game raised $10,000. With that and a bank loan, Friendly House had a new building. Thunderbird Post 41 agreed to share its brand new parking lot, with a little convincing from Diaz.[13]

Through such involvement in the community and after years of hobnobbing with elite Anglos at the Arizona Club on the 10th floor of the Luhrs Building, it's no wonder the charter commission approached him with an idea.

Adam Diaz wasn't simply a good fundraiser. He had also become a trusted leader in his community. He was a property manager of George Luhrs' hotel, and an honorary member of American Legion Post 41. He had organized the first Parent-Teacher Association in his community.[14] He knew influential Mexican American publishers and activists such as Pedro García de La Lama and Jesus Melendrez. Adam Diaz seemed to have been bred for political office. Barry Goldwater hand-picked him to join the 1953 ballot. The candidates and their campaign leader were announced in the summer of 1953.[15]

Adam Diaz was one of seven candidates the CGC had pinned its hopes on. The other names were Margaret Kober, John F. Sullivan, Clarence H. Shivers, Wesley Johnson, Newton Rosenszweig for councilmen and Frank G. Murphy for mayor.

The CGC ticket was off to a running start, benefiting from the late entry in the race by its opponent, the Economy ticket, three weeks before election day.[16]

The two opposing tickets met for a debate on Nov. 6 in which Diaz was cited by the *Arizona Republic* as saying, "There are rumors that if some of the opposition and their supporters have made promises that if they are elected the town will be opened up." This led to a libel case against Eugene Pulliam's Phoenix Newspapers that would not be decided until 1957. The claim was that the newspaper implied Diaz's comment meant the Economy ticket would turn a blind eye to prostitution.[17]

Then, in a blur, the election was over four days later with 11,431 votes cast for Adam Diaz. It was enough to put him in the win column.

On Nov. 10, 1953, 43-year-old Adam Diaz walked onto the political stage as Arizona's first Mexican American city council member. Since Adam Diaz's tenure, there would be six more Latinos elected to the Phoenix City Council: Valdemar Córdova (1955-57); Dr. Ray M. Pisano (1962-63); Frank Benites (1967-69) Armando de Leon (1970-74); Rosendo Gutierrez (1976-80); and Mary Rose Wilcox (1982-90).

Just as swiftly as the run for office had taken Diaz onto the city council, he stepped down. At the end of his term, he decided not to seek re-election because his work was demanding too much of his time. Later he would admit he'd stepped out of the race, "because I felt ill at ease sitting on the council. I believed I lacked the education."

But it would not be the end of his endeavors. Diaz quickly found his way back to community involvement. He helped found an organization called LEAP (Leadership and Education for the Advancement of Phoenix) and joined the Phoenix Elementary School's Board of Trustees. He also would serve on the board of directors for Friendly House, the Urban League, Chicanos Por La Causa and the National Conference of Christians and Jews. He was also a member of the Aging Services Commission.

Educating equally

While the barrios waited for their young men to pass safely through the rigors of the Korean War, they found their younger children struggling to gain a fair education. Despite the fight against Japanese, Nazis and a super-race ideology, the Anglo community seemed to continue its own form of racial elitism in classrooms across Arizona.

The divisions started early in life, namely at school. Hispanic and Black children were separated in classrooms across the U.S. Yet, like slow dominoes, the nation's segregated areas were beginning to fall and build the argument for a landmark case, Brown v. Board of Education.

As early as 1930, Mexican Americans fought for their equality in schools. Independent School District v. Salvatierra was a Del Rio, Texas, case in which a town's school board was sued on the grounds that Mexican American students were not being afforded the same resources given to white students. The district judge ruled in favor of Salvatierra and the Latino students, but the decision was overturned by the state's higher courts on the grounds that there was not sufficient evidence of discrimination in separating the children.

In 1945, the first blow was truly struck by an 8-year-old Mexican girl – Silvia Mendez – in Westminster, Calif. Mendez v. Westminster gained support from a lawyer named Thurgood Marshall, who filed an *amicus curiae* brief. A year later, the case would lead to federal Judge Paul J. McCormick using the Fourteenth Amendment to repeal segregation.[18]

Arizona had earned the worst of reputations for segregation in its school systems. American Indian school segregation was made possible by their relative confinement to reservations and by boarding schools such as The Phoenix Indian School. Arizona legislated some of the most severe segregation of African Americans out of any state in the Rocky Mountains or Pacific West. The educational segregation of Mexican Americans up until the 1940s may not have been as heavily legislated, but it was certainly a de facto practice across the state.[19]

In Phoenix, the struggle wasn't simply for students' rights, nor always in the most obvious places. One veteran, Ray Flores, found his options as a teacher narrowed when looking for employment. After being refused at Anglo schools, he approached Washington Carver High school, a local all-Black school. Even they refused him employment. But this time, he chose to fight minority separation for the right to teach there.

In 1950, Flores became the first Mexican American teacher at Carver High. And the first Mexican American teacher in the Phoenix Union High School District.

As school segregation began to die out, Carver High School closed in 1954. Another member of Post 41 would play a key role in that fall.

A student's request

Throughout the early 1940s, Guy Acuff, principal of Cashion Grammar School, would write numerous articles in the *Westside Enterprise* paper, his words often skewering the status quo of racially-biased education.

In October 1943, a principal in Tolleson drew Acuff's attention. One year after his new promotion, Principal Kenneth R. Dyer was making big changes. He published an article in the *Westside Enterprise* describing how school overcrowding had made his classrooms inefficient and difficult in which to teach. He went on to explain how he had begun to shrink class sizes by putting Mexican children in a separate schoolhouse until they were done with sixth grade. Before this change, the two groups sat separated in one classroom.

Frustrated with Tolleson Grammar School's new segregation of Mexican children for six years, Acuff wrote an open letter in response to Dyer's article to ask, "Is Mr. Dyer's scheme (of segregating classes) merely an administrative convenience or has there been an overall gain in citizenship training as a result?"

He continued to add subtle venom. "Are Mexican American children basically so different from other children that they require specially trained teachers to handle them after they learn English? Will not six years of segregation intensify any antagonistic feelings Mexican children have for children of other parentage?"

It wasn't the first time school segregation had been challenged. At the turn of the century Arizona's Joseph H. Kibbey tried to stop the developing policies of separating Black and brown children from whites. In 1909, as governor of Arizona, he vetoed new legislation to segregate schools, only to see his veto overridden by the state legislature. He went on to serve as attorney for a Phoenix African American family hoping to fight segregation on the claim it did not provide equal educational opportunity for all Arizonans. He won in Maricopa County Superior Court. Then his case was overturned by the Arizona Supreme Court. Kibbey died in 1924, unable to stop the divisive practices he detested.

Kibbey may not have succeeded, but Acuff's concerns would soon receive needed attention.

The Tolleson Grammar School's new Mexican schoolhouse was built at old army barracks north of Van Buren in the West Valley. The original school was a sturdy red brick building on the south side of Van Buren.

One 15-year-old student, Juan Camacho, was not pleased. He decided to take action in 1948. At first the boy tried alone and found no traction in his cause. He needed help. Angelita Fuentes Contreras, Patsy Murrietta and Guadalupe Ramirez Favela, together with Camacho, managed to arrange three entirely unsuccessful meetings with Dyer. The young man still needed more help.[20]

In 1949, he convinced Faustino Curiel Sr., Porfirio Gonzalez, Joe Gonzales (no relation), Isuaro "Chago" Favela, Trinidad Gem Jr., Manuel Peña Sr. and his son, "Lito" Peña Jr., to get involved.

By 1950, they had formed a group called the Movimiento Unido Mexicano (the first of several names). John Camacho was elected president, and "Lito" Peña and Faustino Buriel were part of the Committee for Better Citizenship united forces.

Lito had seen some success already battling the Valley's education system as a member of Post 41. When the post was swamped with complaints in 1947 about overcrowding and double sessions in schools across South Phoenix, post members decided to jump into the fray and find the source of the problem. When they found an unequal distribution of tax levy money, they clashed twice with special interest groups before successfully getting the funds released and spent to help the suffering schools.

In December, Peña, Camacho and several members of the farming community spoke with Kenneth Dyer and the Tolleson Elementary School

Board. The problem seemed to reach an easy resolution when a promise was finally made to eliminate segregation by September.

But in a follow-up meeting the men were told that no such promise had been made and that "if they had, they certainly didn't mean it."[21]

To be better positioned in helping the district, and because Post 41 was overwhelmed with its own obligations at the time, Lito applied for his own post; Post 51 of Tolleson. He was made commander, and meetings were held to plan an attack on segregation.

In February 1950, young Juan Camacho's group signed and sent a letter to Arizona Sen. Carl Hayden in Washington. In the letter they detailed the steps they had taken.[22]

A lawsuit was filed in the name of one of the Mexican American parents, Porfirio Gonzalez, claiming his children were put into a separate school because of their national origin. This was in direct violation of the Fifth Amendment of the Federal Constitution.[23]

The defendant named was the Tolleson Elementary School District 17 board of trustees, led by Ross L. Sheely, Frank Babcock and Principal Kenneth Dyer.[24]

Three people testified: Faustino Curiel Sr., Faustino Curiel Jr., (a student at the time) and Manuel "Lito" Peña Jr.

The Thurgood Marshall-supported Mendez v. Westminster School District of Orange County, decided just four years earlier, was still fresh in legal minds, and provided the basis of much of the plaintiff argument in the Tolleson case.[25]

In mid-November 1950, Judge David Ling was sympathetic to the plaintiff's goals:

"I think the petitioners are correct in their contention that such practices as applied to them are discriminatory. Petitioners are entitled to judgement."[26] But the court rejected their argument of segregation based on nationality, but replaced it with the decision that the school district was actually segregating students by Spanish surname.

A preliminary injunction ruled *"Segregation of school children in separate school buildings because of racial or national origin, as accomplished by regulations, customs and usages of respondent, constitutes a denial of the equal protection of the laws guaranteed to petitioners as citizens of the United States by the provisions of the Fourteenth Amendment to the Constitution of the United States. ... A paramount requisite in the American system of public education is social equality. It must be open to all children by unified school associations, regardless of lineage."*

Tolleson Elementary had to desegregate. "And they didn't. They just kept right on doing it," explains Lito Peña in a later documentary.

"So I called Judge Ling and told him that kids were still being discriminated. And he came into Tolleson and ... brought the United States Marshall with him." The men took a tour of the school district, and the next day discrimination ended.[27]

Unfortunately, desegregating one school did not automatically ensure the rest would follow the same path. But it did start the move toward their goal. In 1952, the Alianza Hispano-Americana's magazine reported that segregation continued throughout Arizona in places such as Glendale,

Miami, Winslow and Douglas. Threats of lawsuits ensued. Glendale acquiesced swiftly by building a new integrated school before the lawsuit could come to fruition.[28]

Another case of segregation at a swimming pool in Winslow interrupted the Alianza's plans to continue its strategies, and the rest of Arizona schools would be slow to follow suit.

At the start of the year, Judge Ling issued his final decree on the Tolleson elementary school segregation case. Months after the January 1952 decision by Judge Ling, Brown v. Board of Education opened. On Dec. 9, in Topeka, Kan., the opening arguments of Brown v. Board of Education were begun. In the course of its proceedings it would cite the Tolleson case. But nobody was waiting for Brown v. Board of Education to be their savior.

As the watershed case continued, segregation activists in Phoenix would push another court challenge through superior court in 1953. In their case, Superior Court Judge Fred Struckmeyer declared segregation unconstitutional a full year before Brown v. Board of Education had been decided.

A new lawyer's star rises

Tolleson's problems seemed to escalate when a Mexican teenager, Jesus Hernandez, was injured by police and arrested for no apparent reason. He was on his way home from Avondale sometime after 9 p.m. Along his route, he saw police officers detaining several others. Curiosity got the best of him. He stopped to watch the commotion. Police were a common fear around Tolleson and other parts of the Valley. They had a reputation for attacking Mexicans, as if for sport.

When Hernandez was spotted, a police officer demanded he get into the police car. As he stepped into the back seat, the group that had already been detained began crying out for him not to comply. He was spooked, remembering the violent notoriety that police had earned. The young man bolted from the police car. He heard two gunshots and ran faster. No bullets ever hit him, but a stone caught his foot and sent him crashing to the ground.

Before he could get up, a police officer struck him over the head. He fell to the ground, and blood began to gush from a four-inch cut in his temple, soaking his shirt. He was taken into custody and sat in a jail cell for 13 hours. A later group of arrested Mexicans stepped into the cell and saw the red stain on his shirt, and pointed out to the guards that he was still bleeding. Finally, he was given medical attention and set free – after his mother paid $45.[29]

The Tolleson Peace Court reviewed the charges made by the arresting officers and found nothing worthy of an arrest.[30]

Valdemar A. Córdova stepped in.

After 18 months as a POW in the German Stalag Luft 1 Berth, he had been liberated and came home with honors in 1945. He married the girl he'd fallen for in 1940, Gloria. Then a fascination with law took him to the College of Law at the University of Arizona in Tucson. There he excelled as a student, won several honors and was elected student body president in 1949. Driven by his studies, he often doubled classes to earn his degree faster. In 1950, his class sat down to take the state bar exam. Córdova finished with the second highest score of his group. In May 1950, the former POW who had grown up near the Grant Park barrio of South Phoenix graduated with a bachelor of law degree.[31]

After his return to Phoenix, he heard the Tolleson boy's story of police harassment. It was an opportunity to put what he had studied to the test. Valdemar Córdova partnered with attorney Gregorio Garcia to file a civil suit.

Córdova and Garcia's civil suit was a success, aided by the absence of Tolleson's presiding justice of the peace. Another, more sympathetic justice from Glendale was called in and ruled that the police officers who had arrested Hernandez would pay $1,000 to Jesus for his damages.[32]

Soon after successfully winning his case in Tolleson, Valdemar Córdova, the activist's son and legal advisor to Post 41, would step beyond the realm of lawyers and eventually onto the judge's bench. But first he would find himself diverted on a political campaign.

Two years after Adam Diaz broke new ground as the first Mexican American on the Phoenix City Council, Córdova would follow in his steps. It was 1955 and the Charter Government Committee's easy successes led them to try again.

Seated is Judge Valdemar A. Córdova with his family in 1959. His father, Luis Córdova, is standing at the far right of photo.

PHOTO COURTESY OF THE CHICANO COLLECTION, DEPARTMENT OF ARCHIVES AND SPECIAL COLLECTIONS, ARIZONA STATE UNIVERSITY

As the campaign began to announce the new ticket, Diaz announced his reluctant departure from the charter committee's lineup. Some in the community attempted to get Diaz to join another ticket, but he would not be swayed from his decision. Diaz approached his close friend, the young lawyer Valdemar, and asked him to be his replacement on the ticket.[33] Valdemar, already a member of the city adjustment board, agreed to join the ticket and was named in August as the charter government's next Latino nominee.

The election proved a simple campaign[34] as mayoral candidate Jack Williams sought re-election, invoking the memories of bad politics in the 1940s. "Would you like to see the city run the way it was in 1948 – before charter government councils and mayors took over?"[35]

After two terms on the City Council, Córdova returned to practicing law in 1958, but he had already made his reputation. By 1959 he was a consultant to the Mexican consulate in Phoenix.[36] He filed suit against Nato Manuel Gloria Jr. and the Garin Bus Co. of Salinas, Calif., in the name of 17 Mexican migrant laborers who lost their lives when Gloria, a substitute driver, fell asleep and careened off the road in South Phoenix. The makeshift bus plowed into a tree and burst into flames. Sixteen died that day. Days later, one more man died of severe burns. Another 31 men were injured.

Judge Ling, who had ordered the desegregation of schools in Tolleson, presided over the case. In March 1960, the young driver was found guilty of gross negligence for having fallen asleep at the wheel.

In 1965, Córdova would achieve a 'first' of his own. He was elected as the first Mexican American superior court judge. He was reappointed in 1966 but quit after a year for personal reasons and returned again to private law practice.[37]

> **Freedom and the rights of man – these are words that are bandied about to the point of complete distortion and misunderstanding.**
>
> **We Americans should keep in mind that in substance our country was founded, prospered and grew in might and power by the recognition of man's one fundamental right – to be let alone.**
>
> **The failure of mankind to recognize that simple fact is the basis for much of the discord and confusion in the world today.**
>
> – Valdemar Aguirre Cordova, 1965

Another decade would pass before Córdova was called on to be a judge once more. In August 1976, Gov. Raul Castro named Valdemar Córdova as a new judge of Division 22 of the Maricopa County Superior Court, replacing Judge Charles Roush who had resigned.

Three years later, upon Sen. Dennis Deconcini's recommendation, President Jimmy Carter would nominate Valdemar Córdova to his highest position yet – a U.S. Federal District Court judgeship in Arizona.

Future Post 41 member and politician Alfredo Gutierrez would recall a cup of coffee he had with Córdova, soon after joining the Arizona Senate in 1972. The young Sen. Gutierrez listened as Córdova "described his role ... and mine at that time ... as the 'convener of the community.' Val never felt he was a leader in the community, and he didn't feel he could pronounce the direction in the community, but he felt strongly that it was important that there be somebody to bring it together. And I think he certainly was that for a number of generations. My generation held him in high esteem."

Steve Zozaya

On the morning after Christmas Day in 1918, Manuela Trebino Zozaya, 23, of Durango, Mexico, received a special gift – a son named Steve Michael.

It was the sixth child for Manuela and her husband Miguel, a section foreman on the Santa Fe Railroad in Kingman, Ariz.

Steve Zozaya grew up with a love of football. At Kingman High School, he earned an athletic scholarship and attended Arizona State College (now known as Northern Arizona University).

But in February 1941 Zozaya set aside the opportunity to be a football star and joined the Army. He became a member of the 158th Bushmasters Infantry Regiment Company G under Capt. Orville Cochran.

Zozaya was there for the Bushmasters' first battle of World War II. Just as the boredom of security duty at the 6th Army Headquarters set in, Company G of the 2nd Battalion boarded a PT boat in January 1944 and headed into the attack on Arawe Island. Zozaya and other star-struck soldiers may have been disappointed by an interesting side note in history.

Their commander, Lt. Col. Fred Stofft, was visited by an old college roommate, Marion Morrison, who had come over with the USO tour to entertain the troops. Stofft walked into his tent and spent the evening talking with his old friend. Then Morrison asked to join one of Lt. Col. Stofft's groups on a patrol. Stofft politely declined. His old roommate had already become known to the world as actor John Wayne. The Colonel "wasn't about to be allow himself to go down in history as the man who let John Wayne get killed."

Steve Zozaya was wounded by mortar fire in the battle for Luzon, earning the Purple Heart. Zozaya also earned a Bronze Star and Company G received the only presidential citation awarded a company during the war.

After the war, Steve Zozaya returned to Kingman where he met the girl of his dreams, Julia Soto. Julia was born to Francisco and Maria Soto in 1926 and grew up on her father's sheep ranch in Kingman. At 19, she married the young veteran and they settled in Phoenix, raising their one son, Steve Jr. Zozaya provided for his family by starting a cement contracting business.

In 1959 Julia's life changed drastically. Retinitis Pigmentosa began robbing her of her sight. But Julia was not one to give up easily. She took a sales position with Sarah Coventry Fashion Jewelry the following year, and graduated from Lamson Business College in 1960. She learned her husband's business and began running the office until an injury in 1966 left him unable to continue the work.

She turned her disability into one of her causes. In 1965 she became vice president of the National Federation for the Blind. In 1975, President Richard M. Nixon appointed her to the President's Committee on Employment of the Handicapped, a position she held until 1981, when a new venture – a radio station – took up her time.

Steve Zozaya took a break from work, but not from his activism. In 1966, he brought the first SER (Jobs for Progress) program to Arizona. Zozaya also served as SER national chairman. Twelve years later the successful program named Steve Zozaya chairman of its national board of directors.

Soon after Julia became the first legally

Col. Alberto C. Gonzalez, veteran of the War in Afghanistan(left), spends time with World War II veteran Staff Sgt. Steve Zozaya (retired) in the hangar of the Arizona National Guard 158th Bushmasters headquarters, amid Blackhawks and Humvees.

PHOTO BY CASSANDRA TOMEI

blind person to get a real estate license in Arizona, she took an interest in her husband's involvement with Latino affairs. During the 1960s, Julia was involved in the creation of a settlement house for Native Americans living off the reservation. She also led a pioneering LULAC study that resulted in housing for Latino senior citizens.

Julia Zozaya became the first national vice president of LULAC in 1965. By 1972, Steve and Julia had held numerous positions with LULAC, including that of state director. Julia decided she would attempt another first for the community: bringing a Spanish-language FM radio station to Phoenix. (Phoenix had two Spanish stations on the AM side).

Julia battled nine years to achieve her goal of snatching up the last unclaimed radio slot in Arizona. The Zozaya-owned company, American International Development, clashed with actor Dick Van Dyke's KXIV Inc. for ownership of the frequency.

The fight seemed lost when the FCC ruled in KXIV's favor, citing its accusations of forgeries by Julie Zozaya on her paperwork. Again she refused to give up, successfully proving that her signature varied due to her blindness.

In May 1981, Zozaya was deemed the "better qualified applicant of the two" and the FCC gave Julia Zozaya permission to operate a 24-hour radio station.

On July 10, 1982, KNNN-FM went on the air. It operated for five years before the cost of the venture overwhelmed the Zozaya's. Julie had put up her father's ranch in Kingman as collateral. They had cut expenses by running the station from their home on Osborn Street. But Phoenix's Latino consumer base had not grown enough to lure advertisers to KNNN. The Zozayas were forced to sell. The radio station became 99.9 KEZ.

Throughout the years, numerous firsts and countless committees, the Zozayas were known for their youthful enthusiasm and open hearts. The couple opened their home to children in need of one as foster parents or helping neighbor's children and runaways who had fled broken homes.

Julia Soto Zozaya passed sway in May 2004 at 78. The local LULAC council 284 of Phoenix was renamed the Steve & Julia Zozaya Council No. 284.

Manny Lugo of Phoenix moves out with fellow troops in Vietnam, circa 1969

1960s

Social change

When the 1950s drew to a close, nobody could have expected the coming changes that would profoundly define the second half of the century. In 1956, Phoenix, Tempe and Scottsdale began expanding and annexing land to increase tax revenue and population, before communities could form identities and incorporate into towns of their own. In 1959, South Phoenix was annexed into the city proper, and many barrios slowly began receiving some of the amenities other communities to the north had enjoyed for so long.

In 1959, the first hints of dissent in Southeast Asia whispered what would become the Vietnam War

With the election of President John F. Kennedy came an escalation of violence. The Viet Cong overran a small forward base during an intense volley of gunfire. Army Sgt. 1st Class Isaac Camacho was taken as the war's first Hispanic prisoner of war. Before completing a second year in captivity, he slipped away to freedom. The Silver and Bronze stars were pinned on his coat in September 1965.[1]

Then on Aug. 2, 1964, the USS Maddox fired on three North Vietnamese torpedo boats in the Gulf of Tonkin. Three days later a Mexican American pilot was taken as the first aviation prisoner, Everett Alvarez Jr. of Salinas, Calif. He would remain captive longer than any other American soldier in the war – eight and a half years. Two years after he was freed, Alvarez Jr. remained in Vietnam. On April 30, 1975, as Saigon fell and American action in the area was abandoned, Alvarez Jr. climbed into the last U.S. helicopter lifting up from the roof of the U.S. Embassy.[2]

In 1965, future Post 41 member Rudy Lopez was in his sophomore year at Phoenix College. Like Henry Daley Jr., Lopez had been struggling with school and strayed into the streets with his older brother. That year would see the first anti-war demonstrations as the draft began pulling men into the U.S. armed forces. Approximately 80,000 Hispanic soldiers would serve during the Vietnam conflict. The year 1965 would culminate with the tragedy of 31-year-old Norman Morrison who immolated himself on the steps of the Pentagon, below Secretary of Defense Robert McNamara's office.

On Jan. 10, 1966, Lopez decided to follow in his family's patriotic footsteps and enlist in the Army. His early days would continue to parallel Henry Daley's experiences and his desire to be on the front lines of Korea 15 years earlier.

"I kinda had to force the Army to send me to combat," Lopez says. "But, by virtue of ... well, I could type 62 words a minute, manual typewriter, with no errors. Then I guess I had a decent head on my shoulders." He went to military school and graduated a personnel specialist. His hopes of active duty in Vietnam seemed to be a sure bet when he was sent to jump school with the 101st Airborne Division at Fort Campbell in Tennessee.

But he was injured as he landed in his first parachute jump and assigned to battalion headquarters as a clerk. It was not what he wanted. He put in a 1049 transfer numerous times before finally contacting Washington to see why he had not heard any response.

Finally, he found that the forms were still sitting in an office at brigade headquarters. He visited the sergeant major, asking to go overseas and fight. It turned out the sergeant major liked Lopez and had grown a bit protective.

"I don't want you to go to 'Nam, because you're the type of guy that's gonna go there and get killed."

But Rudy Lopez would not be deterred. Soon, he found himself back listening to his unhappy superior tell him the news that his persistence had paid off. "Well you done it. I can't stop you now. You're going to Vietnam." Then his superior raised Lopez's pay-grade, explaining, "But the least I can do is make you an E4 – so at least you get killed with a little more money."[3]

Lopez was determined to serve his country, but others were beginning to struggle with the war. Some were outspoken against it. The post itself felt some division, as did the rest of the nation over the validity of the U.S. presence in Vietnam. Younger members such as Alfredo Gutierrez, remember the tenseness in the Ronda Room during the Vietnam era. "We were welcome as long as we kept our mouth shut. If any discussion came up about the war, it was very uncomfortable. We were young.... We liked yelling matches."

Post 41 member Mike Gomez had survived World War II but found the idea of sending his children into battle difficult to stomach. "I had a bitter taste in my mouth when I learned both my sons were drafted for Vietnam. A bitter taste."[4]

It seemed an ongoing curse for his family to be drafted. Gomez did not want to lose his children in this war. Memories flooded back in from dark shadows of the past. He had to stop this.

Sen. Goldwater heard his requests, and made arrangements to send one of his sons home. But it felt too much like choosing one son over the other – Mr. and Mrs. Gomez couldn't make that choice. Both sons remained in Vietnam, thankfully returning home safely from their tours of duty.[4]

The tradition of service

Mike Gomez was one of several Post 41 members who had survived World War II and painfully watched as their sons and daughters marched off to this new war. Many saw their children return, struggling with the experiences of Vietnam. One was World War II veteran Jose Jesus "Chuy" Urias of the Golden Gate barrio. Volunteering to clear the ravaged beaches of Normandy or sweep for mines, Urias saw the blood that war sheds in detail. He was awarded a Silver Medal for taking over a German castle. "I was like a Christmas tree with grenades all over me," Urias recalled in a later interview. "I would say 'cover me' and then I would run."

The Post 41 member had narrowly escaped death in Germany, wounded on the battlefield. But his son, David S. Urias, would not. The Vietnam war took him in April of 1968 at the age of 21.[6]

Others would return from battle with the memories weighing on them both physically and spiritually. Manuel Lugo and Rudy Lopez would both see deep action in small patrol units during the Vietnam War.

Manny Lugo's father, Post 41 member Charles Lugo, was a Marine in World War II, making it through three landings across the Pacific Theater before his fourth landing when shrapnel struck his chest and a bullet caught his leg on the beachhead at Saipan. His father never shared the experiences other than his days flirting with the nurses while he recuperated from his wounds in a Navy hospital.[7]

"That's far as he went. Never talked about the wound, never talked about any of his friends getting hurt. It was all positive stuff. I'm sure going through four landings and when he got hurt. I mean, he must've seen some things that he didn't want to talk about."

Manny also remains vague on his own experiences. He never expected he would go to Vietnam. Three draft notices had come for him, and each time he was turned away. On the fourth notice, he was drafted in 1969.

Lugo shipped off to boot camp in San Diego for 12 weeks.

With a laugh, he recalls, "That was the worst thing that ever happened to me." Then Lugo makes amends with the joke, "Not really. It was the learning experience. But, it was a shock, you know, where they take everything away from you and give you everything you need."

Jose Urias

He easily shares the moments of his arrival and his departure.

After additional training at Camp Pendleton, Lugo and his companions were flown to the front lines. "Commercial airline. With stewardesses. It was just like a regular flight. We left California and went to Hawaii. From there we went to Okinawa. Everybody was happier than hell and having a good time."

Two days later, the men boarded the plane again, on a somber flight to Da Nang, Vietnam. "... A very different trip. Nobody was laughing. Real quiet because we knew where we were going. Even the stewardess. The stewardesses were real quiet. They wouldn't talk as much. It was a whole different deal when we got to Vietnam.[8]

"The nice thing was ... when we landed. When we got to Vietnam the stewardesses gave us a kiss. And they said, 'We'll see you in a year.'"

Lugo spent most of the war 25 miles north of Da Nang for 15 to 30 days at a time. He would stalk the countryside with his small platoon, on patrol for Viet Cong and planning ambushes. "Every three days you'd move to a different position. And it was like a big circle around the base. And sometimes you'd go up into the foothills, up into the mountains. But most of the time our place was up in the rice patties. We were never in the same place for more than three days."

Rudy Lopez shares a vivid moment between his arrival in Vietnam and his return home. Having joined a new group called the Long Range Reconnaissance Patrol (LRRP), he spent much of his time quietly searching the countryside, trained as a medic.

On May 19, 1967, Lopez was one of six men clearing a path down a mine-infested hill. In the delicate effort, their lead engineer slipped up. The explosion tore through the men. Having survived the blast, Lopez attempted to radio back to base.

" ... The handset was blown off my radio. So I couldn't ... as soon as something happens, a firefight or whatever, communication is essential. You need to call somebody and say you've made contact with the enemy, or they know we're here, or something. Tell somebody.

"But with my handset being blown off, I couldn't call anybody. So my next job was a medic. My medic's bag was blown all over the place, so I was trying to pick up bandages or whatever I could find. I crawled over to Ryan, he was the first guy I got to.

"He was a bloody mess from head to toe. His leg was hamburger from just about his hip on down to his knee. I slipped a lot of bandages on him.

"And then, for the leg. All I could do was put a tourniquet. I remembered looking at my watch. It was 11:21. To loosen the tourniquet, I think, every half hour or hour to allow blood to flow back in so you don't get gangrene."

Lopez could feel he was hurt. But he dared not look down. He could only remember his training as a medic. Spotting another survivor, he grabbed the man just as he was going into shock, patching him up the best he could. Then he turned to the lead engineer.

"And I didn't get to him. I was about maybe five feet away when he was face down and he was calling for his mother. And he was crawling. And I noticed the upper torso was moving. And the lower torso. The guy was blown in half."

Lopez had yet to look at his own wounds. Losing blood, he began to pass out. But all he could remember was the words of the medic that had trained him. "Take care of your patients first. Then you."

Finally looking down, Rudy saw his stomach had been torn up and bad wounds to his leg. Falling to the ground, he crawled toward another soldier, Jimmy, to bandage his wounds.

"And Jimmy started firing. We weren't hit, but Jimmy was firing because he was afraid we were gonna get hit. So I crawled and got a weapon. And we were just firing in all directions makin' sure that if there was an enemy out there they knew that we were still alive and kicking, and they ain't gonna take us walkin' in."

After finding a working radio, the three survivors learned they were stranded. All choppers had been engaged into another firefight. Then, a stroke of luck.

"The chaplain just happened to be flying by in his chopper. And I knew the chaplain because I went to see him every

Rudy Lopez in the bush with fellow soldiers.

PHOTO COURTESY OF RUDY LOPEZ

chance that I had. I'd mentioned to the chaplain that I wanted to be a C.A. That was our joke – a chaplain's assistant. And he said, 'Son, no offense, you'd never be happy here. You love it out in the woods.' Yeah but I wanna be a C.A., chaplain!

"So when his chopper landed, I saw him get out the chopper. I looked at him, 'See? I told you I wanted to be a C.A.'"

The two men laughed. Last rites were given to the fallen soldiers and the three survivors were loaded into the helicopter and flown to safety.[10]

Manny Lugo takes a break with fellow soldiers.

Humble in the memory

For their contributions during the Vietnam War, 242 men would receive the Medal of Honor, including 13 Latinos. One of them was Capt. Jay R. Vargas of Winslow. Vargas would bring his Company G of the Fourth Marines through a harrowing night in a village, using fresh graves as trenches, as well as leading his men through a barrage of crossfire and taking out enemy bunkers despite severe injuries.

In a 2008 interview about his own Vietnam experiences, Manny Lugo humbly remembers the day he was given his medal more vivid than the day he earned it. "They gave me a medal. They gave it to me after I got out of the service. They gave it to me right here on 20th Street and Camelback. At Town and Country (Mall).

"They read the reason they … gave me the medal. But it was like, I did something special that particular day, but I don't remember. You do things that you don't think that you're …"

Lugo pauses.

" … It's nothing special. You just do it 'cause you have to do it. And you just react to it. But to be saying that you deserve a medal for that, I don't think that was it … a lot of guys … like … this guy right here."

Lugo points to a framed photo of Silvestre Herrera that hangs on the east wall of Post 41. "Maybe he deserved it, 'cause I've heard his story and it was a special deal … to me it wasn't really something that you were doing special. You were just doing something because you had to do it."

Rudy Lopez echoes his sentiment. He was awarded the Bronze Star for his bravery the day the chaplain's helicopter pulled him to safety. Lopez "refused the Bronze Star for a long time. Because I kept tellin' … Jimmy and Ronnie … I kept tellin' them I was just doing my job. Ronnie would say, 'You saved our lives …' No, I was just doing my job. That's what I'm supposed to do."

Years later, on the fourth attempt, Rudy's daughter convinced him to relent. "Dad! Just get the damn thing. If you don't want it, give it to us. Give it to your grandkids. They want to know what grandpa did."

Rudy found some sense in the words and accepted the medal.

PHOTO COURTESY OF MANNY LUGO

Manny Lugo,
Vietnam 1969

The long road home

When Manny Lugo returned home from 18 months in the rice paddies of Vietnam, he was unable to view life as it was before.

"The guys that I was hanging out with, my brothers and my friends here ... they were still doing the same things that we were doing when we left. And I couldn't get back into that group any more. I wasn't part of that. They were just too different from me. Even my brothers. I couldn't hang out with 'em. I stayed by myself."

Haunted by his experiences in Vietnam, Lugo kept to himself, found employment as a sheet metal worker and raised his family.[10]

Rudy Lopez fought back episodes from his Vietnam days as well. At night, he would fall into the bad dreams, sweating, groaning, agitated. His wife found it dangerous to wake her husband from these nightmares. "The first five years that I was home, it was pretty rough. ... I feel real bad for my first wife because the nightmares were real bad .... My first wife suffered a lot because of my dreams and nightmares."

In the 1970s, Post 41's membership began to shift. The new veterans were looking for a place where they could be with those who understood their experiences.

Manny Lugo had known of the post since childhood. His father among the founding members. After his parents divorced, he would come to the post when he wanted to see his dad. "So I started coming over here. And then I started coming to the dances here. And there was ... it was someplace I could feel comfortable.

"I started seeing some of the guys from the neighborhood. When I went to school, there were members here. And I started getting closer and closer to the post."

Activism comes to town

As Vietnam was splitting the country apart in ideologies, Post 41 continued to stay involved in the barrios. In 1963 it sponsored Boy Scout Troop 119, and offered one of its meeting rooms. Each day, two Boy Scouts would pull down the American flag that flew high above Post 41. They took part in the folding of the flag, and reported to the bartender inside and received an ice cream soda before heading home.

In 1965, the post and its auxiliary also donated more than $5,000 to help nearly 3,000 children in need of welfare. During the summer, the post covered fees for more than 500 children who couldn't afford to swim at Grant Park – repaid by picking up trash around the park to show civic pride. When a report showed less than eight percent of kids in the barrios were able to see a movie, the post spent money to show films at various parks in the community.[12]

That same year, sponsoring a few Little League teams wasn't enough. Post 41 sponsored the entire league and bought the trophies. And at the end of the year, the members and the auxiliary went all out. Christmas had become an especially lively time for the children. More than 500 kids attended the post's Christmas party in 1965, and more than 200 Christmas baskets were given to families in need.

With Post 41 providing basic needs for the surrounding community, some of its members marched into a new stage of activism and success. Valdemar Córdova and Adam Diaz's tenure on the city council had opened doors, but some of the most effective politicians of Post 41 had yet to make their marks.

New Latino activists were sprouting up across the Southwestern U.S. César Chávez and Dolores Huerta co-founded the Agricultural Workers Foundation in 1962. Reies López Tijerina fought to restore land grants in New Mexico. In Denver, Rodolfo "Corky" Gonzales founded his Crusade for Justice and inspired other organizations such as MEChA.

In 1968, as the volatile decade marched toward its climax, Phoenix seemed untouched by the civil unrest that shook the nation. Then Alfredo Gutierrez and several Vietnam veterans returned to Phoenix wanting to speak out against the war and civil injustice. Their Mexican American Student Organization (MASO) began stirring up student protests at Arizona State University. Like many, Gutierrez started humble.

Born in 1945, Alfredo Gutierrez was a miner's son from Miami. The sharp intelligence that would later define him was not as apparent in his youth. Or during his prep years at Miami High School. He holed up in the school library, nosing through philosophy books and the like. When high school was over, he made his escape from the small mining town. In 1962, he joined the Army.

Stationed in Korea, he realized he was at least as sharp as the other soldiers. "The unit to which I was eventually assigned was a mental-health unit, so I was surrounded by people with degrees – doctors, psychologists, social workers. No one in my family had ever gotten a college degree, and until then, I had always assumed that only very brilliant people went to college. The Army taught me that's bull—."[13]

He returned to the U.S. in 1966, thinking he'd settle back into normal life. He married his high school sweetheart, Kathy Castro, and planned to become a copper miners like his father. Then the miners went on strike.

With no work in the small mining town, Tempe seemed as good a place as any for Alfredo's restless spirit. Rather than use his G.I. Bill, he landed a job with the groundskeepers at ASU and worked summers in the mines back home after the strikes were settled.[14]

Before long, he was taking classes and hoping to study political philosophy further than a high school library could take him. But with a sense of organizing and activism, thanks to his father's membership in the mining union, Gutierrez could not ignore the struggles in the Latino community around him. One problem caught his attention. "The laundry that serviced ASU was a major employer of Hispanics in South Phoenix and stories of how people were mistreated there were legendary in the barrio," Gutierrez recalls in a 1991 *New Times* interview.

Soon after, MASO was founded by ASU students and recently returned veterans – some who were already Post 41 members. It took on the laundry firm that worked for ASU. MASO soon was joined by another organization, the Young Socialist Alliance (YSA) formed of extremist Anglos.[15]

In 1968, he became a member of Post 41. In November of that year, there were walkouts. The administration building was overrun and Gutierrez served as a spokesman for the group. Gutierrez was labeled a neo-Trotskyite in an *Arizona Republic* editorial by one of Post 41's older members, Eugene A. Marín.

The results were mixed. Though progress was made, administrators created a disciplinary system to break up future student disruptions. Gutierrez found himself standing before the administrators so often that he was unable to complete classes and quit college. He continued his education through grants from the Ford Foundation and the RFK Memorial Fellowship.[16]

The laundry protests seemed to be the match that set the growing rights movement afire in Phoenix. Soon, Post 41 was lost in a melee of new activism. The call for Chicano power by the Brown Beret movement in Los Angeles was reaching the streets of Phoenix. César Chávez was making the cover of TIME magazine for his march across Southern California to the Mexico border, protesting the use of illegal immigrants to break labor strikes. A local boycott of Phoenix Union High School in September 1970 dominated headlines in Maricopa County for a month. The unrest of the Hispanic community was made well aware to all.

Post 41 had fought for its achievements with the help of local businessmen. Now, however, there were new organizations emerging with out-of-state resources flooding in, such as United Way, to help fight the social issues that were thorns in everyone's side.[17]

The G.I. Forum. LEAP. LULAC. Chicanos Por La Causa. Valle Del Sol Institute. Barrio Youth Project. The Equal Employment Opportunity Program. The Civil Education Project. They all found a niche on which social agenda would focus.

Lito Peña's rise

Before Lito Peña earned his reputation in 1951 for joining the fight against Tolleson's school segregation, he had struggled to find a dream like so many in the barrios.

Lito Peña spent most of his childhood on the west side of town. He was born Nov. 17, 1924, on a cattle ranch in Cashion. He lived there until he was 7 when he and his family moved to Tolleson. He attended Tolleson Elementary School. It was a small school, with Hispanic children on one side and white children on the other. It was like two hemispheres of society. As his eighth grade year was winding down, a teacher (who was also principal) asked the white side of his class to step outside. Once they were gone, he began to explain his version of life to the Hispanic children.

Lito remembers the day the instructor spoke to them. "He said that we were the sons and daughters of farmworkers and that we were destined to be farmworkers, too. He said that there was no need for us to go to high school because we didn't need any more education in the fields."[18] Those words would trouble Lito for several years.

He graduated May 16, 1940, two years before Dyer stepped up from teaching to take the principal's position and separate the children entirely, inflaming the segregation issue that Lito would eventually help eliminate. Peña went on to high school, despite the teacher's words, but dropped out his junior year.

He worked in the fields, picking cotton, lettuce and melons. He then took a job delivering newspapers. In 1944 he moved to El Monte, Calif., to work for a dairy. He returned to Phoenix the same year and took jobs at Reynolds metals and at Luke Field as an apprentice sheet metal mechanic. Lito was gone for a year, drafted into the Army on Aug. 24, 1945, and sent to Seoul, South Korea with the 31st Infantry just as World War II was ending. He was discharged Sept 7, 1946.

Returning home, Lito found he had a new appreciation for his life. He also knew that there weren't any jobs for an 81mm mortar gunner. Manuel began to worry that his grade school principal's unsupportive prediction might come true.

After several jobs, he found stable income as a meat cutter in his father's store. On his off hours and away from his family, he became involved in politics. His community activism began in 1948 when he was a member of CSO, helping to organize voter registration drives. He would also earn his G.E.D. in 1948.[19]

Then Manuel "Lito" G. Peña began to reach for something more.

During the early 1950s, Lito joined with the Community Service Organization. The CSO was born in 1948 out of a desire to increase the number of voters. In 1956, he was appointed the Phoenix representative for the Industrial Areas Foundation of Chicago. During this time, Lito formed some of the foundation blocks of his lifelong fight for employment benefits and unions. These views were further strengthened by a friendship with César Chávez, and that on occasion would put him in direct conflict with Barry Goldwater.

Lito decided it was time to enter politics. Defeat was persistent at first. He lost a race for the House of Representatives in 1960. He failed again in 1962. Then he was asked to try for the Phoenix City Council in 1963. He lost. Three years later, Lito finally won a House seat - by 30 votes. It was 1966.

By the mid 1960s, after founding an American Legion post in Tolleson, he had returned to Post 41. In 1972, when he was elected to the Arizona

Manuel "Lito" Peña during World War II

Senate, he would prove invaluable to Post 41. Tony Valenzuela's eyes light up in an interview when asked about Manuel Peña. A Post 41 member and former national vice-commander, Valenzuela credits Lito for many of Post 41's achievements in recent years. "There's a fine gentleman. Fine, fine gentleman. He helped us a lot. Whenever we wanted something. ..."

Lito would again be a force when Post 41 pushed for a veterans' cemetery with the help of Burton Barr. Tony Valenzuela continues, "We went to state legislature, and we had Lito Peña, Alfredo (Gutierrez) was in there, and guys from other places. And they voted it. We provided money for it."

In 1976, Gov. Raúl Castro would sign a bill into effect providing the funds needed for the state's new veteran's cemetery.

In 1986, Manuel "Lito" Peña would reach national prominence, testifying about a new judge that was to be appointed: William Rehnquist.

An early bumper sticker from one of Mauel "Lito" Peña's election campagns.

Peña vs Rehnquist

On Oct. 28, 1964, a letter arrived for Arizona Gov. Jack Campbell at his office in Phoenix. It was sent by Democratic National Chairman John M. Bailey. The letter warned the governor against organized programs of "voter harassment and intimidation" by Republicans.

He was referring to "Operation Eagle Eye."

In 1962, at Eagle Eye's inception, a young Republican attorney named William H. Rehnquist was the program's point man in Phoenix. Rehnquist and fellow attorneys went to voting stations throughout South Phoenix, questioning minority voters on their rights to vote by asking them to read the Constitution of the United States in English and prove they understood what they had read. Though the Civil Rights Act of 1964 had been implemented four months earlier, it would be another year before the Voting Rights Act gave protection against such illiteracy tests.

In October and November 1964, "Eagle Eye" made national news as the presidential campaign between Barry Goldwater and Lyndon B. Johnson heated up.

With Election Day approaching, national director of the "Eagle Eye" program, Charles R. Barr, announced from Chicago that 100,000 poll watchers in 25 cities would take part, and that 1.25 million voters would be either successfully challenged or discouraged from going to the polls. Barr then dismissed Democratic fears of a "fright campaign."

"No challenges will be made to anybody who is legally entitled to vote. We will challenge anybody suspected of being legally unqualified."[20]

Manuel "Lito" Peña's experience was much different.

He had been assigned a car with a telephone and told to drive to various voting locations in South Phoenix to watch lines and watch for problems. He encountered several lines of voters, most notably in the Bethune voting district of South Phoenix. In several locations he had encounters with men pulling voters aside to demand they recite the Constitution and prove they understood it. At one voting location the exchange grew heated between Lito and one of the men, leaving Lito with a strong memory of that day.

Then in 1971, President Richard M. Nixon named Rehnquist to the U.S. Supreme Court just two years after he had appointed Rehnquist assistant attorney general.

In the 1971 confirmation hearing, Rehnquist was questioned about the suspected harassment of Black voters in the Bethune district during the 1964 election and on pro-segregationist memos as a law clerk to Supreme Court Justice Robert Jackson. Rehnquist admitted directing ballot security programs but denied all claims against him and won his position on the Supreme Court.[21]

It would not be the last time Rehnquist was questioned on his thinly-veiled tendencies toward racism.

About 15 years later Manuel "Lito" Peña spotted a photo in the newspaper and recognized the man with whom he had quarreled in 1964; President Ronald Reagan's nominee to succeed Warren E. Burger as U.S. chief justice, William H. Rehnquist

William Rehnquist in 1972

The confirmation hearing was presided over by Strom Thurmond, a senator with his own checkered past on racial issues. Though Thurmond felt it "unnecessary to go into things gone into before," he relented and three men would testify on voting harassment by Rehnquist. One was Manuel "Lito" Peña.

A portion of his testimony:

"I was a volunteer party worker for the Democratic Party in the general election of November 3, 1964. My assignment was to cruise south Phoenix precincts and western Maricopa County precincts. I was provided an automobile with a telephone. And what I was to do is, whenever I got a call, if a problem existed at one of the precincts, I was to go there and try to resolve it. I was called to Butler precinct. All of this occurred in the morning of that day. I was called to Butler precinct and told to go check a problem; there was a hangup on voting.

And when I got there, there was a long line of people standing outside of the polling place, waiting to get in to vote. The line was four abreast. There had to be about 100 people waiting to get inside the polling place.

I went on into the polling place and asked the inspector what the hangup was. She told me that there was this fellow sitting at the end of the table, and he was sitting at the wrong place, was questioning everybody that came in, and slowing down the process. We had six machines inside of that Butler precinct, and only two of them were being utilized as a result of the slowdown of voting. I told the inspector that the proper thing to do would be to take the challenger and whoever he is challenging and move him to a corner of the building; let him ask all the questions that he wanted to; and allow the rest of the people to vote, instead of questioning the voter in line, holding up the other people from voting.

The fellow objected to this. And at that point I stepped in between him and

the people who were moving into the line, and I told him, you are in the wrong place as a challenger. You should be behind the inspector, and you should only challenge if you have a good cause to challenge.

He was asking everybody who came in what their name was, where they lived, how long have they lived there, that kind of thing. I told him that was not a legal way to challenge. And he said he wanted to make a telephone call, so I took him into the principal's office – Butler is a school – and he made his call.

I do not know who he called. But after talking to somebody for a few minutes, he told me that he was told that what he was doing was correct, and that he was going to continue to do it. And I told him that he was not going to do it because it was not the correct way to challenge. He could challenge if he wanted to if he did it in a correct manner.

At any rate, he insisted that he was going to do it again. He went back into the polling place. My job was to call back to headquarters and tell them what had occurred, and they would send somebody out to take care of the problem.

When I did that, I was given a message to go to another precinct and check another problem there. I returned to Butler precinct about 30 or 40 minutes later, and the line had diminished, people were voting. I went inside the polling place and asked the inspector what had happened.

And she said that somebody came in and had an argument with the challenger, physically removed him from the polling place, and had a conversation with him outside, and the fellow disappeared. And so we had kind of a peaceful election after that at that polling place.

Now, later – a few years later – I saw a picture in the paper of William Rehnquist. And I recognized him from that picture as the person who was doing the challenging inside the polling booth, inside the polling place, and who was impeding the traffic of voters into the booth.

And that is how I came to know that Mr. Rehnquist was involved."

After the statement, Lito was questioned briefly by Democratic Sen. Edward Kennedy of Massachusetts. Then he was questioned on the minutiae of his encounter by Republican Sen. Dennis DeConcini of Arizona, Democratic Sen. Howard Metzenbaum of Ohio and Republican Sen. Howell Heflin of Alabama.

Utah Sen. Orrin Hatch bluntly questioned him, "You did not know him from the man in the moon. Is what you are saying? Is that right?"

After Peña responded, "I do not know the man in the moon either," The two pretended they could not hear each other, and the sharp exchange was smoothed over.

After a televised grilling of Rehnquist by senators Kennedy, Joe Biden and others, the vote came in. William H. Rehnquist became the 15th chief justice – though the 65-33 vote marked the largest negative tally ever received by someone confirmed to be Chief Justice.[22]

First duty: grab a mop.

Tony Valenzuela has energy. And he's not afraid to speak his mind. His enthusiasm and drive have helped him become State Commander of the American Legion, and National Vice-Commander. One more step and he could have been the Legion's president.

But that would have meant too much traveling around the country.

Valenzuela has known of Post 41 since his college years in 1948. "I had uncles and cousins and everything else, who had been in the military, and they belonged to Post 41 at that time. So they used to bring me in here, even when I was not eligible to come here."

One uncle was Roy Yanez, the director of the Marcos de Niza Housing project.

But Valenzuela also remembers the division that took years to fade. As the founders of Post 41 watched new veterans from new wars return, the post became divided at times. "A lot of problems within ourselves. We've always (had) a certain resentment against each other. Like Lencho's World War II. Lencho didn't like me 'cause I was a Korean veteran. And Korean veterans didn't like guys from Vietnam." It's a clash that he regrets happened, and is thankful has faded with time. He also remembers clearly walking into Post 41 after returning from the Korean War.

"When I first came in here, they had just completed the Ronda Room. A guy says, 'Who are you?'

"I say, 'My name's Tony. I just got a discharge and I'd like to join Post 41.' I had on my uniform.

"And one of these guys said 'Well, why would you wanna do that?!'

"I said, 'Simple. I've been here before. I know what it's all about. Now I'm eligible, and I wanna join!'

"And I had stripes you know? I had a bunch of stripes — I was a staff sergeant. And I said, 'I think I can do something.'

"And they looked at them stripes and said, 'Well, *what* can you do?'

"Any thing! I'm capable. I can do any thing." 'You really wanna join post 41?'

"Yeah."

Suddenly one of the men put a mop in Tony's hand.

"What the hell you doin'? I wasn't in the Navy! I was in the Air Force. Can't you tell the difference?"

During the exchange, a man stood there watching and waiting — sizing up the younger veteran. It was Ray Martinez.

"Ray Martinez, loved him… loved him. He's standin' there lookin at me. Watchin me. I says 'well, what do you think?'

"He said 'Well…gotta start somewhere.'

"I say, 'Ok.' And I grabbed the mop and … started mopping."

Later, the two men would become the best of friends.

The members of Post 41 celebrate in the 1950s

Ray Martinez with Senator Barry Goldwater at American Legion Post 41 in 1984.

Left to Right, Dennis DeConcini, Ron Murphy, John McCain and Ray Martinez together in 1987.

1970s – Present

On the battlefield

When President Richard M. Nixon took office in January 1969, he became the fourth president to handle a troubling Vietnam War. It was not to be a quiet end to the decade either. At the start of the year, Harvard was seized by protesting students. By year's end, hundreds of thousands were protesting across the nation. Social unrest had not only taken hold in the U.S., but Sudan and Libya were each overtaken in government coups. Curaçao and Malaysia, El Salvador and Northern Ireland all saw rioting. Hurricane Camille wrecked the coastlines of Mississippi, Alabama and Louisiana. And Charles Manson's cult sent Los Angeles into shock with the murders of several prominent citizens.[1]

That year a study was released, examining Hispanic participation in the Vietnam War. The study compared Hispanic casualties during two stretches of time: January 1961 to February 1967, then December 1967 to March 1969.

The study found a combined 8,016 casualties from the states of Arizona, California, Colorado, New Mexico and Texas. Almost 20 percent had Hispanic surnames – nearly double the 1960 census at 11.8 percent in these five states. The Hispanic contribution may have been even higher, but the study had excluded two key states with a substantial Hispanic population – Florida and New York.[2]

The findings were significant because Hispanics made up just 10 percent of the country's population. The research also revealed that many Latinos were involved in higher risk branches of the service, such as the U.S. Marine Corps.

The Hispanic contributions and the price of their involvement were heavy, but there was also an unspoken price. As science learned how to save more lives on the battlefield, many more soldiers returned from the war with lost souls and lost limbs.

Thunderbird Post 41 would start the new decade with a loss of its own. One of its founders, former post commander Tony F. Soza, passed away of a heart attack in August 1970. Despite 70% disability from grenade blast injuries in New Guinea during World War II, Soza had remained active. Only two years before passing, he had been the Arizona District commander. The post voted to change its name in his honor. Thunderbird/Tony F. Soza Post 41.

With so many other organizations taking up causes and achieving success, Post 41's political-social involvement became quieter in the 1970s. It still served as a gathering point and a heartbeat for the barrios, along with places such as Sacred Heart Church and the Calderon Ballroom.

Individually, the post's members continued to broaden their success. Post 41 member Steve Zozaya was elected state director of LULAC. Zozaya and his wife, Julia, would later own the first Spanish-language F.M. radio station in the valley, KNNN Radio.

The charter government powerbrokers had helped five Latinos get elected to the Phoenix City Council, starting with Adam Diaz in 1953 and Valdemar Córdova in 1956. Optometrist Dr. Ray M. Pisano served from 1962-63, Air Force Gen. Armando De Leon would serve from 1970-1974, and Rosendo Gutierrez from 1976-1980.

The city changed to a district system and the Charter Government Committee that had helped Latinos gain political clout and office for 30 years was fast becoming an outdated organization. Rosendo Gutierrez threw off its support and won his second term as an independent. Margaret T. Hance was elected the second female mayor of any major U.S. city.

The population had grown 10 times what it was in 1950, and few in the city remembered the political climate of the 1940s when the CGC was created.

Modern Phoenix was emerging. While there would be lingering issues of racial equality, the city had become a major metropolitan area. By 1980 it was the ninth largest city in the U.S. and still growing.

Alfredo joins the senate floor

In 1969, one year after the laundry walkouts at ASU, Alfredo Gutierrez was instrumental in organizing Chicanos Por La Causa, an organization that within three decades would be known as the second largest Latino nonprofit in the U.S. Gutierrez also worked as program director for Barrio Youth Project in South Phoenix.

Gutierrez won a Ford Foundation fellowship and made plans to take classes at the University of Maine. He was hoping to study under a political philosopher that he had grown to admire, and toyed with the idea of becoming a teacher. But the boredom of summer played havoc with his loose plans.

Gutierrez noticed an election approaching. Suddenly, he felt the urge to run for office.

Alfredo Gutierrez in 2005

PHOTO BY PHIL SOTO

He announced his bid to run for a senate seat against District 23's Cloves Campbell. Gutierrez did not expect to win. He printed thousands of flyers, citing Campbell's high absentee rate and lack of involvement. Manuel "Lito" Peña pitched in a help to his campaign, and the flyers "went like hotcakes."

"The incumbent had been in office a long time. He was an executive with APS, and in my opinion was totally out of touch with the needs of his constituents," Gutierrez recalls. "People in my district really depended on the county hospital, and it was common at that time for a person to wait hours to see a doctor."[4]

By a mere 136 votes, Gutierrez defeated Cloves Campbell, the African American incumbent who had held office since 1966 – and the first African American to do so in Arizona. Campbell would mount numerous comeback attempts, forcing Gutierrez to constantly battle for the position he had earned.⁵

The clout and legacy of Post 41 can also be seen in 1993. Alfredo Gutierrez rejoined Post 41 when he saw Rudy Lopez had rejoined. Though he had often worked in the same circles with South Phoenix communities, Gutierrez was an example of the power in Post 41's growing legacy. Where Ray Martinez and Pipas Fuentes founded the post and went on to make change, Gutierrez, who had first joined in the 1960s, made his name, and then was drawn back to the post by its legacy.

A quiet time and loss of community

"You know, I've been known for a long time as a bad boy and I want to thank you all for closing your eyes to that," the elderly man spoke from his wheelchair. Bishop Edward McCarthy had just heaped praises on during a Mass. It was two days before the 4ᵗʰ of July 1975.⁶

After Mass concluded, the old man was surrounded by hundreds of his friends congratulating him on 60 years of service to the Catholic Church. His weathered skin was proof of what he had given to the people of South Phoenix, what he had given to the Mescalero Apaches of New Mexico. And as a Japanese POW during World War II.

Looking down at his swollen feet, Father Albert Braun spoke again. "I've been wanting to die for a while, but God won't have me and I don't like the other place, so I just keep hanging on."

With a sigh, he mused quietly, "I used to be a hard worker in those days."

The mid-1970s were not an easy time for many in South Phoenix. Some Latinos reached new heights in the Valley, and yet many were suffering low blows.

The most notable high was Raul Hector Castro. He finally succeeded, on his second attempt, at what many could not have expected so soon. In 1976 the Tucson native became the first Mexican American governor of Arizona.

The same year Castro announced his second run for governor, the city of Phoenix was preparing for expansion of its airport with an environmental impact study. The final report described a relocation program to move people out of the largely Mexican-American barrios to make way for the airport. High unemployment rates and low property values in the barrios were cited as reasons the program would prove successful.

The study ignored the disruption this plan would cause. Developers and city officials moved forward with the proposals. In June 1977, a notice in the *Arizona Republic* announced Phoenix would start buying properties to the west of Sky Harbor and razing them. As property values in the area plummeted further, the residents were often taken advantage of. Some stood firm, refusing to move, but the community was collapsing around them.

In 1981, Golden Gate was declared a slum and wholesale demolition of

A senate ribbon from 1975

IMAGE FROM CHICANO COLLECTION, DEPARTMENT OF ARCHIVES AND SPECIAL COLLECTIONS, ARIZONA STATE UNIVERSITY.

the community began. The barrio would be just one of several sacrificed for the desires of a city and its airport. Communities continued to fall, house by house for another three decades, until just a few last bastions remained, such as Sacred Heart Church, American Legion Post 41 and a few streets of old homes tucked away, unnoticed.

One of the barrios' most valiant defenders, Father Albert Braun, could only sit by and watch, confined to his wheelchair after heart surgery in the early 1970s. In 1982, God finally took Father Albert Braun at the age of 92. His beloved Sacred Heart Church was boarded up three years later.

Another of Post 41's bright stars was extinguished on June 18, 1988, when Valdemar Aguirre Córdova died. He had retired four years earlier after suffering a stroke. One of the last high profile cases he presided over was the 1982 decision that ended a political fight to redraw district borders in Arizona.[7]

As the barrios faded around Post 41, the legionnaires began to focus more on veteran's affairs.

Then, one after another, the founders passed on. Frank "Pipa" Fuentes would also pass away in 1982 at the age of 73.

On Dec. 3, 1993, Ray Martinez was laid to rest. After his active years as the commander of Post 41, he was elected Arizona District Commander in 1950. He had spent most of the following decades working to improve the lives of children as the legion's children and youth chairman.

In 1988, Post 41 co-founder Lencho Othon was elected Arizona district commander and succeeded in mobilizing Arizona legionnaires in a push to gain a national veterans' cemetery. The 225-acre cemetery, dedicated in 1978, was finally transferred officially into VA control and renamed the National Veterans' Cemetery of Arizona on April 1, 1989.

Into the 1990s Lencho Othon continued his efforts with involvement in the development of a new Arizona Veterans Home, opening in November 1995 next to the Carl Hayden VA Hospital in Phoenix. Just months after the facility opened, it was at risk of closure. As co-chair of the legion's District 12 Rehab Committee, Lencho joined in the successful effort to convince the city to apply for new funding.

In 1993, Post 41 immersed itself in the task of organizing a memorial that was to be erected in honor of Father Albert Braun, who had died a decade before. A Father Braun Committee was formed to handle the logistics, which included the acquisition of three large stones. One came from the Philippines, where Braun had been captured during World War II. The second was to be shipped from the Mescalero Apache reservation in New Mexico, where Braun had helped the tribe construct its church in the 1920s and 30s. The third was a stone from Yarnell. Artist Carlos Ayala was contracted to create the sculpture.

The post's reputation was recognized nationally for its work with communities and the voice it gave veterans. One of its members, Tony Valenzuela, was named commander of the Arizona Department of the American Legion.

A 1993 statue of Father Albert Braun in Wesley Bolin Memorial Park, Phoenix, Arizona.

PHOTO COURTESY FRANK BARRIOS

"Post 41 is probably the best recognized and respected post in the whole country. Now, being that I've traveled all over, I know. And people have asked me. They say, 'Hey. I see you're from Post 41. I'd like to go. I've heard so much..'

"Well you come over." Valenzuela would respond. All are welcome.

Post 41's biggest benefit? It was there for those veterans who could not find a kindred soul that might understand what they had seen in battle.

Along a highway

On Aug. 2, 1990, Sadaam Hussein invaded the small, oil-rich country of Kuwait. The U.S. moved swiftly, launching Operation Desert Shield to protect against a possible invasion of Saudi Arabia, where they had interests in the oil reserves.

In 1990, the U.S. fought the Persian Gulf War. By now the Hispanic inclusion in the military was far-reaching, with about 20,000 Latino service men and women deployed in Operation Desert Shield and Desert Storm.

Post 41 member, Adam Hernandez watched the attack unfold on the evening news, thinking, "Ahh, man ... there's gonna be a real thin possibility I'll get activated. Transportation. I thought we were just a small unit that they probably wouldn't call us. We're, like, 130 guys."

He had already served in the Marines as early as 1975. After a break from the military, he signed up again in 1985, this time with the Army National Guard. "After 5 years back, I still wanted to serve again. The national guard seemed like a good thing to do for the community. That's why I joined." He was listed with the 220th Transportation Division. Thinking it was a small division, he didn't believe he'd be called.

In September, he was activated and sent to Fort Huachuca for training in Operation Desert Shield. The sudden activation took Hernandez by surprise. "Things happened so fast. Soon as we got called up, we went and started training at Fort Huachuca. And we trained there and by November we were in Saudi Arabia.

Adam Hernandez in 1976

"I didn't really realize how involved we were in it until we were flying into Saudi Arabia in a commercial airline and a couple F16s pulled up to the side of the aircraft we were flying in and escorted us down to the Saudi Arabia airport. And that's when it hit me that this was serious."

Adam Hernandez never fired a shot in the Gulf War, but what he saw struck him deeply, nonetheless. "When we went towards Kuwait, we went down the 'Highway of Death.' There was a lot of pictures of that in the magazines, to get to 'Camp Freedom' up there. It was right after the Iraqis were trying to get out of Kuwait. They took the highway, and they were attacked by the aircraft.

"A lot of destruction. A lot of bodies ... just ... A lot of destruction."

Adam Hernandez
in Kuwait, 1990

A long pause. "I thought about the horrors of war. Seeing actual destruction of human life ... um ... kinda felt ... almost guilty about ... you know, the soldiers that I saw there. The Iraqi soldiers. I know I didn't personally ... attack them, you know, with my own weapons, but ... I felt like I was still part of it because it was U.S. forces. There was a lot of grief about it in me for a while.

"A year. Almost a year we were over there. We were one of the first units in there to move everybody in. And of course, we were one of the last units to leave because we were transportation."

Like Manny Lugo and Ruben Lopez who returned from Vietnam struggling with what they had seen, Hernandez would find some comfort through the VA. And through Post 41.

A hundred guys ... or one

By 1979, Puerto Rican Horacio Rivera had risen to the rank of full admiral in the Navy, the first Hispanic to reach that rank in the U.S. armed forces since Spaniard David Glasgow Farragut in the 1860s. In 1982, Richard E. Cavazos became the first Hispanic four-star general. Nationally, Latinos were reaching for the highest positions.

The same year Rivera was named a full admiral, Latino Edward Hidalgo became secretary of the Navy. Before and during the 15 months he would serve this post, Hidalgo advocated for more Latinos in the military. He changed the face of recruitment campaigns. Television ads targeted Latinos. Well into the turn of the century, the Marines and the Navy would remain the top choice for Latinos enlisting in the armed forces.[9]

But by 2003, when the U.S. entered Iraq again, there was a growing change among the Latino soldiers' demographic. In March 2003, Major General Freddie Valenzuela attended a funeral for the first casualty of the Iraqi War. The young soldier, Army Spc. Rodrigo Gonzalez-Garza, had not yet received U.S. citizenship.

There seemed to be a new focus on poverty levels and citizenship of U.S. soldiers. A 2005 article started the conversation by citing rough vernacular for the troops that now had joined the armed forces for economic improvement or to achieve U.S. citizenship; 'working class mercenaries, green card troops, non-citizen armies, or desperate recruits of the U.S. government's 'poverty draft.'"[10]

After the tightening of U.S. border restrictions and empowerment by a 2002 executive order from President Bush, the armed forces made promises of citizenship to new recruits. The article continues to cite the results: By

2004, between 31,000 and 37,000 troops out of a total of about 130,000 were non-U.S. citizens serving in the Navy, Marine Corps, Army and Air Force.

And yet, as the military was gaining more soldiers, the American Legion was losing its veterans. Post 41 was no exception. Despite these new veterans, Post 41 has struggled to maintain its membership. Indeed, the entire organization. In 1996, the organization announced it was losing 30,000 members worldwide a year.

Former post Commander Henry Daley is aware of the difference. "I think I felt more like coming here than they do now. So many other things to do in this town. Back in 1954, there wasn't that much. There were maybe three or four dance halls or places that they had music. The legion being one. And the Riverside and Calderon (ballrooms).

"And that was about it. Now they have so many places to go to."

But the camaraderie and community awareness at Post 41 seem to have become a very special bond to both veterans and their families. And though soldiers had been known to show preference to veterans of their own wars, the 1970s showed a broad inclusion at Post 41 that continues to this day.

The Gold Star Mothers and Sisters of Post 41, with help from the Auxiliary Women's Post, has helped with the sorrow of fallen soldiers for more than 50 years. And they do it on their own. The National Gold Star Mothers organization, founded in 1928, does not have a local chapter. Mary Moraga has been a member since her brother died in Korea in 1951. Each year the organization holds a Memorial Day service in honor of their fallen soldiers. "To me, it (Memorial Day) has always been special. So many young men died. My brother was one," she says holding back her tears.[11]

Rudy Lopez had left the post, unhappy with the rift he saw between older veterans and Vietnam vets. As time had gone on, Vietnam veterans had become more involved in the post and carried the legacy into the present. Rudy decided to return, unable to resist the connection he felt at Post 41. "A lot of heritage. A lot of Hispanic heritage. I left Post 1. It's a real good post. That post is mainly Anglo. When I got there, the Adjutant said 'I heard about you, you're a troublemaker, huh!?' I said, 'Nope, nope. I just wanna be a member and ... I won't do anything.' The adjutant says 'no, that's what we want. We want members asking questions. We want fresh eyes. You see anything wrong, you let us know.' And true to their word, they did. At Post 1, I was accepted. But my heart was always here.

The Post 41 Women's Auxiliary visits the National Memorial Cemetery of Arizona each Memorial Day.

"Now we're unifying. Now we're doing things."

Many survivors of these wars, such as Vietnam veteran Manny Lugo, cannot imagine having found a safer haven than Post 41. His steady voice grows passionate when he thinks of Post 41 and what it has meant to him.

"I'm just glad I found this post here. Every time I walk in here, if there's a hundred guys in there or one guy, you know ... you're a friend. It feels comfortable. It's like a family. I'm not saying they're closer than my family, but. I see' em more often. And it's more comfortable coming over here than going anywhere else.

"I wish everybody could have a place to go to that was what this is to me. This is my home. Well, you probably have some place that you go, and everybody knows you and they shake your hand and give you a little hug and they treat you right. And that's what this place is for me.

"And... I tell some of the older guys ... they built this place here. They made this place for us. And now it's our turn to give back to them by keeping this place maintained. Keeping it going. And telling them thanks for giving a place to come over to."

Post 41 turns to its own ranks

Some have carried the Post 41 tradition and made their membership a family affair. Chandler city council member Martin Sepulveda related in a newspaper article that his father, a Korean War veteran, would often meet him at Post 41 to hang out. Years later, after a tour of duty in the 1991 Gulf War, Sepulveda joined. "Thinking back, it must have been the assortment of characters, veterans of World War II, Korea and Vietnam, who made these visits memorable. All were proud of their service to this nation.

"It wasn't like I was planning on being a regular there, living in Chandler, but it was an opportunity to become part of a veteran lineage that isn't replicated anywhere else in the state. I've maintained the tradition of taking my son to be with these unsung American heroes at least twice a year. He's a corpsman in the Navy Reserves, serving with a fleet Marine force unit."[12]

In November 2005, then-post commander Robert Peralta explained bluntly the difficulties Post 41 faced in achieving some of its goals. "A lot of people have been dying off, and we've been trying to recruit new members."[13]

Between 1995 and 2005, the post lost more than 100 veterans of World War II and the Korean War. In May 1998, one of the post's closest friends and an honorary lifetime member, Barry Goldwater, passed away at 89.

Henry Daley remembers the week of his death. "I was commander at the time. So we wanted to do the honor guard for him. It was pretty hard to get in to talk to somebody about doing that. I went down to the church he belongs to there on 3rd Street and Roosevelt. Goldwater's wife quickly stepped in and allowed the men of Post 41 the honor of the first in to pay their respects.

"So we were the first ones allowed into the church before the other people came and we walked in. All the members. We walked in and we paid our respects to him and saluted and paid our condolences to the wife. Then we went to their auditorium. Mrs. Goldwater came in. We all saluted her. She came and thanked all of us."[14]

Tony Valenzuela also recalls the day and considers it one of the post's more treasured moments. "His wife made sure that before anybody went through that, the members of Post 41 went through there first. We were honored to say goodbye to Barry."

Into the new century, the post remains a gathering place of Latino pride. LULAC has continued to have its local meetings there and in 2005, their national convention convened there.

Then the time came for the community to turn around and do something for the post that had worked so hard for it. It was time to save Post 41's legacy. It was time to save the legacy for all Latino veterans.

Full circle

Fifty years after the opening of Thunderbird Post 41, the world has changed and evidence of its founders' achievements is fading.

The 158th Bushmasters no longer hold their fall reunions. It is no longer feasible. Too many have passed away over the years.

The original desegregated swimming pools of Tempe Beach have sat empty since 1975. They were then demolished in 1998 to make way for Tempe Town Lake and Park.

In April 1996, the gavel sounded and Arizona's regular senate session came to an end. Manuel "Lito" Peña's long political career was ending as well. He was stepping down after 30 years seated in the state House of Representatives.

Even the post's coveted $1-per-year lease agreement with the city was nearing its end after 50 years. Suddenly the post seemed at risk. In 1997, the lease was extended another 15 years, but as the city entered a multi-billion dollar renaissance of development in its central district, the venerable Post 41 was vulnerable as a property with non-historic designation. (At the publication date of this book, just three year remain on this new lease).[15]

In 1997, members renegotiated a 15-year lease extension with the city. At the time, thoughts of purchasing the property from the city were brought up. But a shrinking membership meant shrinking dues. They didn't have the money.[16]

In 2005 Phoenix city council member Michael Johnson told reporters that there were no plans to uproot Post 41. And as the U.S. economy hit rough waters in 2008, the post may have been saved from the jaws of property investors and developers.

To shut the doors of their building would have been a tragedy of Phoenix heritage. But voices were already beginning to speak up in defense of the South Phoenix icon and of the unspoken contributions made by Latinos in the U.S. war efforts of the 20th century.

At the University of Texas, an associate professor of journalism, Maggie

Rivas-Rodriguez, noticed a large hole in the story of World War II. An estimated half million Latinos seemed to be missing from the histories that comprised one of the most important events of the 20th century.

She also saw that the opportunity to have those stories told was fading. Time was short, and these guardians of lost history were in their sunset years. Rivas-Rodriguez moved quickly to fill the gaps. With the U.S. Latinos & World War II Oral History Project, she began to compile stories from Latinos across the United States that had experienced the war.

In 2006, the materials collected by Rivas-Rodriguez's project became resource material for a play portraying their stories. "Voices of Valor" told the story of Latinos who returned from World War II to fight for their rights at home. It was performed onstage in Tempe and in Austin, Texas.[17]

Then an increased urge to defend and honor the heritage of Latino soldiers in World War II became a roar. When Ken Burns released a documentary called "The War" in 2007, many Latinos spoke out over the absence of their story. Burns acquiesced by tacking a new Latino segment to the end of his documentary, but several other documentarians would produce videos of their own.

One of those documentaries, "Los Veteranos," had been filmed by the son of a Post 41 founder before the controversy of Ken Burns' "The War." Dr. Pete R. Dimas is a historian and professor who was able to get his documentary aired on the local PBS station, KAET Channel 8, following airings of "The War." The story of Post 41 was now being shared with an entire community that had grown up, unaware of its accomplishments.

As Phoenix enters a new era, the South Phoenix area is poised to enter a renaissance as the memory of floods and factories and segregation have begun to disappear. Comfortable in the land's desirability, Phoenix dropped the need for flood insurance requirements in many neighborhoods in 2008. New development plans have emerged for the vacant land around Sacred Heart Church. A massive rental car facility was constructed in 2004, and South Phoenix barrios continue to disappear. Few bastions of the barrio legacy remain in Phoenix. One is Post 41.

Post member Manny Lugo is just one of many who refuse to let Post 41 fade into memory.

"I think it's important to give something back to the old timers that made this place for us. I wanna keep this post going.. This post should be going to the end of time. And I think it's important to open our arms to the guys that are coming back from Iraq and Afghanistan. Just like the Vietnam guys when they came back, they weren't welcomed openly."

That love and respect for the founders of Post 41 carries forward. Ray Martinez' daughter Norma Kiermayr shares a moment when her two sons returned from duty during the second Iraq war in 2003. They had been members since the first Gulf war in 1990.

"They walked into Post 41 and the bartender asked them, 'Can I help you?' They said 'yeah we'd like a drink?' When the bartender explained it was a membership only place, they pulled out their American Legion cards."

When they were asked how they came to be members, they explained their grandfather's name was Ray Martinez.

With that, the bartender brought their drinks – and refused to let them pay for anything they ordered that day.

Though the sound of gunfire has stilled...

On Nov. 26, 2007, in Glendale, a family member walked into Silvestre Herrera's bedroom to wake him for breakfast. He did not respond. One of the icons of Arizona's military pride had passed away, one month shy of his 91st birthday.

Arizona claimed him as its hero. He was a regular in Memorial Day parades throughout the years. Post 1 made him a member when he returned.

But it was Post 41 he called home. Here, he was with men who knew him as a member of the community, not just a hero. They had all been through battles, both against enemies abroad and at home. At Post 41, he could still hear the echo of barrios he had known since 1928.

Nine days before Silvestre Herrera passed away, he granted an interview to Sgt. Benjamin Cossel of the military publication, *Desert Sentinel*.

"You can never feel sorry for yourself," Silvestre explained. "I've never let anything be an obstacle. When I couldn't walk, I crawled. I don't cry for my legs. I never did. They're gone, they don't care."

And so it was with the veterans of Post 41. The struggles of their barrios and the tragedies served to bring them together more as Latinos. It united them to fight for the American Dream, be it in war or at home.

Still to this day, Post 41's mission statement stands relevant. It bears repeating as the first 60 years of Post 41 conclude, and the next 60 begin.

> *"Ever since it can be remembered, Americans of Spanish speaking ancestry have striven to promote the welfare of our country to uphold and defend its constitution and to fight for it proudly in time of war. It is not intended to drop the battle of justice, freedom and democracy merely because the sound of gunfire has stilled."*

To my value friend
Ray Martinez, first elected
Commander of American Legion
Post 41 and State Comm
With regards
Sgt. Sil

Resources

INTRO

1. *Minorities in Phoenix*, by Bradford Luckingham
2. *Corridors of Migration*, by Rodolfo Acuña, pg. 48
3. *Abraham Lincoln and the Western Territories*, by Ralph Y. McGinnis, pg. 86
4. *Corridors of Migration*, by Rodolfo Acuña, pg. 48
5. *Arizona Republican*, Feb. 19, 1891
6. *Los Veteranos* documentary, by Pete R. Dimas
7. *Minorities in Phoenix*, by Bradford Luckingham, pg. 25
8. *Arizona Republican* Aug. 8, 1914, pg. 1; Aug. 9, 1914; Aug. 10, 1914
9. *Arizona Republican* Sept. 15, 1914
10. *An Awakened Minority*, 2nd edition, by Manuel Servín, pg. 116
11. *Corridors of Migration*, by Rodolfo Acuña, pgs. 218-9
12. *Arizona: A History*, by Thomas E. Sheridan, pg. 214
13. *Journal of Arizona History*. pg. 14, Spring-winter 1973 "Minority group Poverty in Phx" by Shirley J. Roberts, pg. 353
14. *Arizona: A History*, by Thomas E. Sheridan, pg. 217
15. *Minorities in Phoenix*, by Bradford Luckingham pg. 40
16. *Minorities in Phoenix*, by Bradford Luckingham
17. *Los Veteranos* documentary, by Pete R. Dimas
18. *Minorities in Phoenix*, by Bradford Luckingham, pgs. 35-40
19. *Los Tucsonenses*, by Sheridan, 102-12, 166-79; Carlos C. Jácome, clippings files, Arizona Historical Society, Tucson; Meeks, "Border Citizens," 102-16, 267-69, supported by many Mexican-Americans.
20. *Los Veteranos* documentary, by Pete R. Dimas
21. *The U.S. Mexican border in the 20th century* by David E. Lorey. Pg 72
22. Letter from director of Friendly House, Placida Garcia Smith to Maricopa County Board of Supervisors, July 11, 1933, Hugh C. Gilbert Papers, 1914-1933, MS 1097, Arizona Historical Society, Tucson; "Placida Garcia Smith," 80-81, Arizona Women's Collection, Department of Archives and Manuscripts, University Libraries, Arizona State University, Tempe, Arizona.
23. *Minorities in Phoenix*, by Bradford Luckingham
24. *Border Citizens: the Making of Indians, Mexicans, and Anglos in Phoenix* by Eric V. Meeks.
25. *Minorities in Phoenix*, by Bradford Luckingham
26. *Minorities in Phoenix*, by Bradford Luckingham
27. *Los Veteranos* documentary, by Pete R. Dimas
28. *Saving Private Aztlan: Preserving the History of Latino Service in Wartime. Diálogo Magazine*, by D. López. July 14, 2006

1940s – the war

1. *Hispanics in America's Defense*, Diane Publishing Co. pg. 2
2. *Hispanics in America's Defense*, Diane Publishing Co.
3. Interview with Norma Kiermeyr by author
3. *Los Veteranos* documentary, by Pete R. Dimas
4. *Los Veteranos* documentary, by Pete R. Dimas
5. *Progress and a Mexican American Community's Struggle for Existence*, by Pete R. Dimas orig. quote Carey McWilliams, North from Mexico: the Spanish speaking people of the U.S. (Philadelphia: JPB Lippincott Co. 1949, pg. 259 and Christine Marín's "Mexican Americans on the home front: Phoenix in World War II, 1981
6. *Arizona Republic* "Castro names former judge to court post" Aug. 27, 1976 and article "Old school ties," Nov. 29, 1982, also En Az Quien es Quien? (Arizona Who's Who) Phoenix: Fiesta Productions, pg.16
7. *Los Veteranos* documentary, by Pete R. Dimas
8. Interview with Mike C. Gomez, by Christine Powers, Univ. of Texas Oral history
9. *Arizona Republic* Nov. 10, 2005, and University of Texas. Interviews.
10. *Los Veteranos* documentary, by Pete R. Dimas
11. Ibid.
12. Ibid.
13. *Az Men/Women of World Warr II* by Christine Marín, also *Hispanic Historic Property Survey* by David R Dean, Jean A Reynolds, Historic Preservation Office, Phoenix (Ariz.), Athenaeum Public History Group, pg. 69
14. *Profile in Heroism; Medal of Honor Recipient, Silvestre Herrera* by Sgt. Benjamin Cossel, Operation Jump Start - Arizona Public Affairs, 2007
15. *Arizona Republic* "Herrera's moment of unparalleled courage" Sept. 25, 2005
16. *Arizona Goes to War*, by By John (FRW) McCain, Marshall (INT) Trimble
17. *Arizona Goes to War*: by John (FRW) McCain, Marshall (INT) Trimble
18. *Los Veteranos* documentary, by Pete R. Dimas
19. *Los Veteranos* documentary, by Pete R. Dimas
20. *"We Made Our Life As Best We Could With What We Had: Mexican American Women in Phoenix, 1930-1949"* by Reynolds, Jean A., M.A. thesis, Arizona State University, 1998, pg. 113
21. *Progress and a Mexican American Community's Struggle for Existence*, by Pete R. Dimas, pg. 113
22. *Progress and a Mexican American Community's Struggle for Existence*, by Pete R. Dimas, pg. 113
23. *Arizona's Hispanic Military contribution"* by Christine Marín Chicano Archives

24. Ibid
25. *Hispanic Historic Property Survey* by David R. Dean, Jean A. Reynolds, Historic Preservation Office, Phoenix (Ariz.), Athenaeum Public History Group, "Americanization and Mexicans in the Southwest: A history of Phoenix's Friendly House, by Mary Ruth Titcomb, pg. 59, also *El Mensajero*, Oct. 9, 1942, also *Progress and a Mexican American Community's Struggle for Existence*, by Pete R. Dimas, pg. 110, also *Arizona Republic*, Nov. 27, 1942, section 2
26. *Progress and a Mexican American Community's Struggle for Existence*, by Pete R. Dimas, pg. 110
27. Marín pgs. 5-6
28. *V Amphibious Corps*, Appendix 3 to Annex C to Operation Report, Occupation of Japan, Nov. 30, 1945, pg. 31
29. *Arizona Republic* "Latino vets share their story" March 11, 2006
30. *The price of democracy, Arizona Republic* May 31, 1999
31. *Progress and a Mexican American Community's Struggle for Existence*, by Pete R. Dimas, pg. 109
32. *Los Veteranos* documentary, by Pete R. Dimas
33. *Yuma Daily Sun*, Sept. 7, 1945, "Large fund raised for Hero of WWII"
34. Interview with Mike C. Gomez, by Christine Powers, Univ. of Texas Oral history
35. Interview with Ralph Amado Chavarria, by Erin Dean, Univ. of Texas Oral history
36. *Arizona Republic* March 19, 1946 "Veteran, family beaten by mob" pg. 6
37. *Los Veteranos* documentary, by Pete R. Dimas
38. *Arizona Republic* March, 31,1980, "Hispanic American Legion Post Fights Against the Powers That Be"
39. *Hispanic Historic Property Survey* by David R. Dean, Jean A. Reynolds, Historic Preservation Office, Phoenix (Ariz.), Athenaeum Public History Group, pgs. 90-91
40. Ray M. Martinez, personal interview with Jean Reynolds, Tempe, Arizona, Nov. 16, 1999. Tempe: Arizona Historical Society.
41. *Hispanic Historic Property Survey* by David R. Dean, Jean A. Reynolds, Historic Preservation Office, Phoenix (Ariz.), Athenaeum Public History Group
42. Interview, Joe Torres by Pete R. Dimas
43. Interview with Pete R. Dimas and Lencho Othon, Horizonte, KAET Ch. 8, 2004
44. *Phoenix Gazette*, Jan. 24, 1948 "Hectic climax session crowns ring champions"
45. *Grant Park Weekly Tribune* 1948 ASU Chicano Archives
46. Interview by author with Norma Kiermeyr
47. Interview by author with Norma Kiermeyr
48. *LULAC and Veterans Organize for Civil Rights in Tempe and Phoenix, 1940-1947* by Christine Marín
49. Letter in Chicano archives, rm-244 ASU Chicano Archives
50. *Tempe News*, April 18, 1942; "Week's Doings," Tempe News, Sept. 10, 1942 "Today's Local News"
51. *Mexican Americans On the Home Front: Community Organizations in Arizona During World War II"* Perspectives in Mexican American Studies 7 by Christine Marín. (1993): 83, also in LULAC and Veterans Organize for Civil Rights in Tempe and Phoenix, 1940-1947 by Christine Marín
52. "LULAC and Veterans Organize for Civil Rights in Tempe and Phoenix, 1940-1947 by Christine Marín. ASU Chicano Archives collection
53. "LULAC and Veterans Organize for Civil Rights in Tempe and Phoenix, 1940-1947 by Christine Marín. ASU Chicano Archives collection 26.
54. "LULAC and Veterans Organize for Civil Rights in Tempe and Phoenix, 1940-1947 by Christine Marín. ASU Chicano Archives collection
55. "LULAC and Veterans Organize for Civil Rights in Tempe and Phoenix, 1940-1947 by Christine Marín. ASU Chicano Archives collection
56. Ray M. Martinez. Personal interview with Jean Reynolds, Tempe, Ariz., Nov. 57. 16, 1999. Tempe Historical Society
58. Barbara Crumpler, president, Beta Phi Chapter, Arizona State College, Tempe, to Tempe Beach Committee, (CHSM-570). Chicano Research Collection. Department of Archives and Manuscripts. University Libraries. Arizona State University, Tempe, Ariz.
59. Ray M. Martinez. Personal interview with Jean Reynolds, Tempe, Ariz., Nov. 60. 16, 1999. Tempe Historical Society.
61. Letter in ASU archives, from files of J. O. Grimes, dean of the college, Chicano Archives
62. "LULAC and Veterans Organize for Civil Rights in Tempe and Phoenix, 1940-1947 by Christine Marín. ASU Chicano Archives collection
63. *Arizona Republic*, May 22, 1946. "Policy Changed at Tempe Pool," also "LULAC and Veterans Organize for Civil Rights in Tempe and Phoenix, 1940-1947 by Christine Marín.
64. *Arizona Republic*, Oct. 24, 2003, pg. 10 "Pool symbolizes segregated past"
65. "LULAC and Veterans Organize for Civil Rights in Tempe and Phoenix, 1940-1947 by Christine Marín. ASU Chicano Archives collection
65. Solliday interview, Tempe Historical Museum archives
66. KAET Ch. 8 interview, Arizona stories
67. Quote by Ray Martinez in *Arizona History* and Feb 26, 1946, *Arizona Repubulic* pg. 5 "Housing Unit work started"
68. Quote by Ray Martinez in *Arizona History*
69. Ibid, also see Towards Metropolis Status: Charter Government and the Rise of Phoenix, Arizona, 1945-1960 by Konig, Michael F., Ph.D. diss., Arizona State

University, 1983, pg. 190, footnote 3
70. *Arizona Republic*, July 3,1946 "Federal Housing project Scrap Rages at Hearing"
71. *"We Made Our Life As Best We Could With What We Had: Mexican American Women in Phoenix, 1930-1949,"* by Reynolds, Jean A., M.A. thesis, Arizona State University, 1998, pg. 58; Ray Martinez in Arizona History
72. *Hispanic Historic Property Survey* by David R. Dean, Jean A. Reynolds, Historic Preservation Office, Phoenix (Ariz.), Athenaeum Public History Group, pg. 74
73. *The Emerging Metropolis; Phoenix 1944-1973*, by William S. Collins pg. 47
74. Ibid
75. Ibid
76. *Arizona Republic*, July 4, 1946, pg. 1, "New House Project Hit By Owners"
77. Ibid
78. *Arizona Republic* July 6, 1946, pg. 1, "Controversial Vets Project Is Supported"
79. *Arizona Republic*, July 7, 1946, "Work Start is Set For Vet Homes"
80. *Arizona Republic*, July 10, 1946, "Group tells opposition to vets housing"
81. *The Emerging Metropolis; Phoenix 1944-1973*, by William S. Collins pg. 266, also *Hispanic Historic Property Survey* by David R. Dean, Jean A. Reynolds, Historic Preservation Office, Phoenix (Ariz.), Athenaeum Public History Group, pg. 75
82. *Progress and a Mexican American Community's Struggle for Existence*, by Pete Dimas, pg. 12
83. *Hispanic Historic Property Survey* by David R. Dean, Jean A. Reynolds, Historic Preservation Office, Phoenix (Ariz.), Athenaeum Public History Group, pg. 73
84. *Los Veteranos* documentary, by Pete R. Dimas
85. *Los Veteranos* documentary, by Pete R. Dimas
86. Letter from Ray Martinez, 50th anniversary celebration booklet, Post 41 Chicano Archives
87. *Race work:* by Matthew C. Whitaker
88. Pulled from interview with Lencho Othon by Pete R. Dimas on *Horizonte*, KAET Ch. 8, also *Hispanic Historic Property Survey* by David R. Dean, Jean A. Reynolds, Historic Preservation Office, Phoenix (Ariz.), Athenaeum Public History Group, pg 91
89. *Arizona Republic*, Nov. 10, 2005:
90. *"American Legion Post #41. Presented at the 2003 Historical convention."* by Jean A. Reynolds, also Ray Martinez biography files ASU Chicano Archives
91. *Horizonte* transcript, KAET Ch. 8
92. *Arizona Republic*, Nov. 10, 2005
93. *Phoenix Gazette*, Jan. 20, 1946
94. *Arizona Republic*, March 14, 1948
95. KAET Ch. 8 transcript: Norma Kiermeyr interview.
96. *Tucson Daily Citizen*, May 24, 1961. "Enduring values of this land" By Barry Goldwater
97. *Hispanic Historic Property Survey* by David R. Dean, Jean A. Reynolds, Historic Preservation Office, Phoenix (Ariz.), Athenaeum Public History Group, pg. 103
98. Hispanic Historic Property Survey by David R. Dean, Jean A. Reynolds, Historic Preservation Office, Phoenix (Ariz.), Athenaeum Public History Group, pg 93, also from 50ᵗʰ Anniversary event program, American Legion Post 41 archives
99. Interview with Tony Valenzuela, by Author
100. *Arizona's Hispanic Flyboys* by Rudolph C. Villarreal, also *Tempe Daily News* April 29, 1949, pg. 1
101. Interview with Florencio Othon, by Author
102. 1980 District Convention booklet, ASU Chicano Archives
103. *Hispanic Historic Property Survey* by David R. Dean, Jean A. Reynolds, Historic Preservation Office, Phoenix (Ariz.), Athenaeum Public History Group

1950s
1. *Moberly Monitor Weekly*; Nov. 29, 1950, pg. 1, col. 4
2. Interview with author, Oct. 15, 2008
3. Human Ecology Review, Vol. 12, No. 2, 2005, pg. 159, "The Geography of Despair: Environmental Racism and the making of South Phoenix" by Bob Bolin, Sara Grineski and Timothy Collins
4. *Arizona Republic*, Jan. 16, 1961
5. *Los Veteranos* documentary, by Pete R. Dimas
6. *Yuma Daily Sun*, Feb. 18, 1954 pg. 2
7. Interview with Lencho Othon and Pete R. Dimas, *Horizonte*, KAET Ch. 8
8. *Minorities in Phoenix*, by Bradford Luckingham, pg. 28, also *Arizona Republic*, Oct. 12 and 13, 1914, also *Arizona Gazette* Feb. 3, 1914
9. *The Emerging Metropolis; Phoenix 1944-1973*, by William S. Collins, pg. 45
10. *The Emerging Metropolis; Phoenix 1944-1973*, by William S. Collins, pg. 54
11. *The Emerging Metropolis; Phoenix 1944-1973*, by William S. Collins, pg. 50
12. Pete Dimas interview ASU Chicano Archives, also *Arizona Republic*, Aug. 31, 2003
13. *Arizona Republic*, April 27, 1977, pg. 1 Section C
14. *Arizona Republic*, Jan. 4, 1954, pg. 2, col. 1
15. *Arizona Republic*, July19, 1953, pg. 14, col 1
16. *Tucson Daily Citizen*, Nov. 11,1953, pg. 30, col 4
17. *Tucson Daily Star*, June 1, 1957, pg. 2, col. 4 "Court reverses Libel Suit against Paper," also *The Emerging Metropolis; Phoenix 1944-1973*, by William S. Collins pg. 65
18. *Chicano Education in the Era of Segregation*, by Gilbert G. Gonzalez, pgs. 136-

156. The Lemon Grove case, described by Robert Alvarez in *Familia*, also illustrates the unity and resolve of the Mexican American community in Lemon Grove, Calif. (48-49,152-55).
19. *Frontiers Journal*, 1999, *"This is not right": Rural Arizona women challenge segregation and ethnic division, 1925-1950*, by Mary Melcher
20. Letter from Sonny Peña to Michael Murphy in *Arizona Republic*, ASU Chicano Archives e-392, criticizing the errors of an article and of the naming of a school.
21. ASU Tolleson Library E-392
22. Letter to Sen. Carl Hayden, Tolleson school segregation folder, at ASU Chicano Archives E-392.
23. *Arizona Republic*, Nov. 23, 1950, "Spanish segregation in school barred"
24. Gonzales v. Sheely, 96 F. Supp.1004 (D.C. Ariz. 1951)
25. *The Promise of Brown v. Board of Education: In Commemoration of the 50th Anniversary of Brown v. Board of Education*, March 2005, Arizona Attorney General Terry Goddard
26. *Arizona Republic*, Nov. 23, 1950, "Spanish segregation in school barred"
27. *Los Veteranos* documentary, by Pete R. Dimas
28. *An Awakened Minority*, 2ⁿᵈ edition, by Manuel P. Servín, pg. 180
29. *El Sol*, April 11, 1952
30. *El Sol*, Dec. 22, 1950
31. Biography; Córdova, Val 1983, ASU Chicano Archives
32. *El Sol*, April 11, 1952
33. *Arizona Republic*, July 14, 1955, pg. 1
34. *Arizona Republic*, Aug. 9, 1955, pg. 1, col 5
35. *Arizona Republic*, Nov 5, 1955, pg. 1, col 1
36. *Arizona Daily Sun*, June 17,1959, pg. 11, col. 4
37. *Arizona Republic*, Aug. 27,1976, "Castro names former judge to court post"

1960s
1. The First Marine captured in Vietnam, by Donald L. Price, 2007
2. U.S. Department of Defense files
3. Interview with Rudy Lopez, by Pete R. Dimas at Post 41, Oct. 15, 2008
4. Interview: Univ. of Texas oral history project, by Christine Powers
5. Interview: Univ. of Texas oral history project, by Christine Powers
6. Newspaper clipping from Post 41 archives, *Arizona Republic* 1968
7. Interview with Manny Lugo, by Pete R. Dimas at Post 41, Oct. 15, 2008
8. Ibid
9. Interview with Rudy Lopez, by Pete R. Dimas at Post 41, Oct. 15, 2008
10. Interview with Manny Lugo, by Pete R. Dimas at Post 41, Oct. 15, 2008
11. Interview with Rudy Lopez, by Pete Dimas at Post 41, Oct. 15, 2008
12. *Arizona Days and Ways* magazine, Dec. 4, 1966
13. *New Times*, Feb. 6 1991, by Kathleen Stanton
14. *Arizona Republic*, June 13, 2005 "Alfredo Gutierrez," also *New Times* 1991
15. *Chicano!*, by Francisco Arturo Rosales, pg. 212
16. *New Times*, Feb. 6, 1991
17. *An Awakened Minority*, 2ⁿᵈ edition, by Manuel P. Servín, pg. 250
18. Bio, Peña, Manuel "Lito" E-392, ASU Chicano Archives
19. Bio, Peña, Manuel "Lito" E-392, ASU Chicano Archives
20. *New York Times*, Nov. 3, 1964, "Democrats Charge G.O.P. Poll Watch Today Will Harass the Negroes and the Poor"
21. *Las Cruces Sun-News*, Nov. 22,1971, pg. 2
22. *Tucson Daily Citizen* Nov. 1, 1971, pg. 18, also *New York Times*, Oct. 30, 1964
25. Cabell Phillips, "G.O.P. Opens Drive to Prevent Fraud"

1970s - Present
1. *Hispanics in America's Defense*, Diane Publishing Co., pg. 39, also *An Awakened Minority* 2ⁿᵈ edition, by Manuel P. Servín, pg. 2.
3. *Star News*, July 7, 1971
4. *New Times*, 1991
5. *Arizona Republic*, Jan. 19, 1975
"Senate majority leader faces key challenge at 29"
6. *Arizona Republic*, July 3, 1975,
"Ex-POW priest is honored at mass for 60-year- career
7. *Kingman Daily Miner*, April 2, 1982
8. Interview with Adam Hernandez, by Pete R. Dimas at Post 41, Oct. 15, 2008
9. Department of Defense, *Population Representation in the Military Services, Fiscal Year 2004*.
9. *Arizona Republic*, 2005 Gold Star Moms Keep Alive Memories of Fallen Soldiers
11. *Life Lottery: U.S. military targets poor Hispanics for frontline service in Iraq*, in New Internationalist, May 2005, by Richard Hil
12. *Arizona Republic*, Nov. 9, 2007 "To those who put their lives on the line for U.S.: Thank you"
13. *Arizona Republic*, Nov. 10, 2005 "An army veteran who fought in Vietnam"
14. Interviews with Tony Valenzuela and Florencio Othon, by author, Oct. 15, 2008
15. *Arizona Republic*, Nov 10, 2005
16. *Arizona Republic* , Nov 10, 2005
17. *Arizona Republic* March 11, 2006

Index

A word from the Raul H. Castro Institute

The Raul H. Castro Institute is honored to co-publish *The Faces of Post 41* with Latino Perspectives Magazine. We believe that it is of the utmost importance to document the contributions of U.S. Latinos from Arizona who served during World War II. This document highlights in an eloquent and compelling manner the participation of many individuals of Latino descent in the war effort. Many served and some were casualties and, with this document, we preserve their stories for future generations. The recognition of the individuals from Post 41 and other U.S. Latinos had been neglected in the extant histories of World War II.

It is our hope that this book will result in a fuller appreciation of the contributions of various ethnic groups to our common interests. We enthusiastically co-publish this book to commemorate the individuals whose lives are showcased herein and so that neither the young nor old of our community forget an inspiring chapter of our collective history. Their courageous performance on the battlefield contributed to victory for the U.S. and its allies; their tenacity and desire for social change in Arizona upon their return helped shaped our sense of identity and purpose as a community.

Trino Sandoval, Ph.D.
Acting Director,
Raul H. Castro Institute

A word from Latino Perspectives Media

Latino Perspectives Magazine was founded in 2004 with the purpose of creating a better understanding and more accurate portrayal of the Latino community in the state of Arizona. We document our community's rich cultural diversity, its accomplishments, challenges and many contributions.

For more than 200 years Americans of Latino descent have contributed to shape Arizona. *The Faces of Post 41* tells a story of a remarkable group of young American Latinos who were called on to protect our liberty and defend our country and came home to a community that did not fully accepted them as fellow Americans and took their service for granted.

This book is the culmination of a year-long project that has sought to recognize the work of individuals who, with dedication, pride, and without fanfare, serve our community and make it a better place in which to live and dream.

We salute the men and women of American Legion Post 41 and those who have contributed to their mission along the way. Thanks to their sacrifice and unwavering commitment to justice and social equality, our community is more diverse and inclusive.

Together with our partners Salt River Project and the Raul H. Castro Policy Institute we are proud to present his book to public libraries and high schools in our state so that students in Arizona can learn about the contributions of extraordinary Americans of Latino heritage. It is our hope that this book will inspire inquiring minds to cherish and participate in the transformational power of volunteerism and community service.

Ricardo Torres
CEO
LPM

Cecilia Rosales, Ph.D.
COO
LPM